COME REST

Learning to Let Jesus
Love You and Lead You

RICHARD F. SPEIGHT, JR.

COME REST

ISBN: 978-1-886296-50-3

Published in the United States by
Arrow Publications
P.O. Box 10102
Cedar Rapids, IA 52410
Telephone: (319) 395-7833
Toll Free: (877) 363-6889 (U.S. only)
Fax: (319) 395-7353
www.arrowbookstore.com

To John + Diana
with all my love
Dick Speight
1/25/09

RECOMMENDATIONS

"Until the message of Come Rest was deeply in my spirit, I found myself constantly striving to love others and win the lost out of my insecurities. Learning to first rest in the Father's love as my position of strength for everything else I do has radically altered my family life, ministry and destiny!"

Caleb Plumb
Pastor, Encounter Christian Church
Cedar Rapids, Iowa

"Richard Speight has a vital message for the churches of our time. Too often we think it's up to our efforts to make ourselves into effective disciples of Jesus and that we need the 'right model' to make our church relevant. This book is a grace-filled call to fall deeply in love with Jesus, to spend time with Him, to be molded as humble followers of the One who does the work of transformation. In a distinctly prophetic spirit reminiscent of St. Francis and John Wesley, Richard makes it clear that when we rest in God's love, we become vessels of the Holy Spirit who remakes the world through our lives. This is all God's doing, not ours. The genius of this remarkable book is that when we allow our souls to stop striving and begin resting in God's love, then and only then is the power of God unleashed in the world to overcome social injustice and bring the transforming work of God to families in conflict, the oppressed, nations in chaos, and the poor."

Pastor Will Jackson
Presbyterian Missionary
Cedar Rapids, Iowa

"With such unrest in our world, Jesus' great invitation of 'Come Rest' is truly a crucial message for this hour. In following a portion of Richard's agonizing journey in writing this book, I am not surprised at the depth, clarity, practicality, and simplicity of this work—because he trusted Jesus. His message is changing my life."

Steve Russell
Pastor, Jordan Grove Baptist Chruch
Central City, Iowa

"We live in a 24/7, non-stop, always connected, relentlessly busy world that leaves us more empty and alone than when we found it. Only God has a remedy for us. God has made Richard a rich blend of a desert father, an evangelical contemplative, and a loving pastor. The result is a message that provokes you from all sides to rest in Jesus. 'Come Rest' is more than a book; it's an invitation into the life of rest you were designed to live."

Travis Kolder
Church Planter, Cedar Rapids House Church Network
Cedar Rapids, Iowa

"This highly inspirational book gives credible witness to the author's call and lived experience of resting in Jesus. The reader comes away deeply motivated to let Jesus love us and lead us in this quest to rest in Him."

Sister Nancy Hoffman FSPA
Prairiewoods Spirituality/Ecology Center
Cedar Rapids, Iowa

"'Work hard, play hard' is the mantra of a generation hopelessly striving to outrun our fear, anxiety and pain—and we are EXHAUSTED! Come Rest is not a 'stop and smell the roses' message, but rather insights into the real, freeing truth that finally gets us to where we've wanted and needed to go all along."

Glenn Shields
CEO, Graham-Shields Strategic Forums
St. Louis, Missouri

"Richard Speight has detailed a biblical remedy for a chronic condition in the body of Christ. Epidemic levels of unbridled busyness have overtaken the spiritual rest of many people of God. Without the intervention of a call to rest such as this, we may find ourselves rich in schedules and programs but with our hearts in a desert of turmoil. We must take the medicine now, allow the peace of the Lord to renew our minds, and emerge deeply at rest in HIM."

Ric Lumbard
Director, Wind and Fire Ministries
Marion, Iowa

This book is lovingly dedicated to the memory of my mother,
Janetta Ann Speight, and in honor of my father,
Richard Forrestt Speight, Sr.—
loving, sacrificial parents who treasured each other and
introduced me and my dear brother, Steve, to Jesus!

Acknowledgements

I thank the Lord for His arms of love.

Emily Speight for hard work, clarity and loving insight as
editor and cover designer (besides being such a great daughter
and powerful handmaiden of the Lord!)

Lila Nelson for tender care and counsel as proofreader.

Victoria Fink and Arrow Publishing for encouragement and
expertise in the home stretch.

Francis Frangipane and the pastors and people of
River of Life Ministries for standing with us in the journey.

My nephew Jamin Nollsch for the photo used in the cover.

Faith Bible Church and Pastor Steve Benton for providing us
housing in the first months of our ministry
as I began writing this book.

My son Daniel for always cheering me on.
I'm #94's biggest fan.

My in-laws Merilee and Arnie, our wonderful extended family
and friends for lots of hugs, laughs, and prayer!

Last, but not least, my beloved "Bright Eyes."
Kim Speight, life is simply beautiful because of you.

Richard Speight
November 2008

CONTENTS

PART TWO: LETTING JESUS LEAD YOU

FOREWORD

By Francis Frangipane

I have known Pastor Richard Speight for almost ten years. Besides being a close friend, I have known him to be a man of integrity. He's a man who lives out the role of a servant and finds delight and power in walking humbly with the Lord.

Over the years, I've seen the Holy Spirit bless Richard with a growing and successful church. I've also watched and stood with him as the Holy Spirit has tested him during trials. In all things, I have found Richard to be a man who steadfastly places his trust in God. The lessons he shares in *Come Rest* are living realities, truths that he has personally experienced. His prescription for life's stresses have found their first fulfillment in Richard himself.

Richard's soul rests in the goodness of the Almighty. Like the swallow, Richard has made his nest at God's altar (Ps. 84:3). From his dwelling place in God's presence, he urges the reader, "Come rest" in the love of God.

INTRODUCTION

Rhythms of Rest

Get away with me… I'll show you how to take a real rest… Learn the unforced rhythms of grace… Keep company with me and you'll learn to live freely and lightly.

— *Matthew 11:28–30, MSG*

Come rest in My love! This is Jesus' great invitation for this hour. We live in a fearful time of great shaking. We are weary from terrorism, gas prices, politics, immorality, natural disasters, stock markets, and wars. We are fearfully exhausted from striving for security, and we are failing. But this is not a bad thing. Jesus is not worried. The end of our self is the beginning of Him.

Jesus says, "Come to Me, all you who labor and are heavy laden, and I will give you rest. Take My yoke upon you and learn from Me, for I am gentle and lowly in heart, and you will find rest for your souls. For My yoke is easy and My burden is light" (Matt. 11:28–30, NKJV).

Jesus sees your weary heart. He invites you to stop striving and begin thriving. He offers Himself and three rhythms of rest for your daily lifestyle: Come to Him, take His yoke, and learn from Him. He wants you to live freely and lightly. It's why He led you to this book.

15

COME REST

Rest is not "taking a break." Rest is unbroken company with Jesus.

The Bible says, "All who confess that Jesus is the Son of God have God living in them, and they live in God. We know how much God loves us, and we have put our trust in his love" (1 John 4:15–16). Rest is trusting His constant love to be enough for your constant trials.

Here's real Christianity—learning to let Jesus love you and lead you. Come rest from running your own life. Let Him be your security and destiny. Come rest from trying to fix yourself or others. Be filled with His power. Stop making Jesus follow you and begin truly following Him.

The purpose of this book is to help you come to Jesus, resting in His love as your lifestyle and your identity. You will find Scriptures, stories, and principles to help you *let* Jesus love you and *let* Jesus lead you. You can't *let* Jesus lead you until you really *let* Him love you. When you stop and *let* Him love you, He can begin to heal you, free you, and lead you—thereby releasing His love through you to a desperate world.

Sooner or later, we all get tired of trying on our own to make life work. The load of leading yourself through life will eventually grind you into the ground. You don't have to carry that load anymore. You don't have to live under all the old layers of fear, expectation, ambition, restlessness, grudges, and shame. Someone else wants to be responsible for your life—Someone who really loves you and really knows what He is doing—Someone you can trust.

When reading this book, rest and let Jesus speak to your heart as He chooses.

Be loved.

Be led.

Come rest.

PART 1:

LETTING JESUS LOVE YOU

CHAPTER 1

RESTING SECURE

I've cultivated a quiet heart. Like a baby content in its mother's arms, my soul is a baby content.
— *Psalm 131:2, MSG*

One Sunday morning, after a worship service, I approached some visitors during snack time. A toddler was safely nestled in her father's arms, eating a cookie. She had chocolate all over her face. She looked deeply into my eyes, and then she pulled the mushy cookie out of her mouth, offering it to me. YUM!

How intently generous! How messy—but how intently generous! I will never forget the lesson. If she had been wandering alone in the midst of towering strangers, she might have been frightened or confused when I approached her. However, safe in her daddy's arms, she could look me in the eyes and offer me that which was most dear to her at the moment.

This is the Lord's desire for us. It is a picture of His people at rest in Him—at His return. Are we secure children of the Father, joyfully giving our lives away for the lost and the poor? Let's not wait for His return. Let's return to His embrace, look deeply into the lives of others, and give them all *He has* for all they need.

Not ready for that? Are you all stirred up with the cares of this world? You can begin by spending time looking deeply into His eyes.

But you can't look deeply from a distance. He is not pointing a finger at you, He is just opening His arms. Let go of what holds you back. Run to Jesus. Stumble, crawl, fall—whatever! As you rest in Him, you will grow more *content with Him*. Then you will be able to freely give His gifts to others.

Jesus and His disciples were on the Temple grounds one day when He saw a perfect illustration of secure giving. "Then he saw a poor widow put in two pennies. He said, 'The plain truth is that this widow has given by far the largest offering today... she gave her all!' " (Luke 21:2–4, MSG). This account of the "widow's mite" is often trivialized, even by the use of the phrase itself.

Jesus was reaching into the disciples' hearts by pointing to the widow's generosity. He was redirecting their focus onto His kingdom. However, they quickly drifted away and began to fixate on the beautiful stonework of the Temple and the memorial decorations on the walls.

Isn't that just like us? We hide from the hand of God by admiring the handiwork of humanity. We trade love and mercy for bricks and mortar. We trust strategies rather than the Spirit. We preach doctrine instead of the Gospel. We pursue our own self-interest rather than God's glory. And the last barrier we hide behind is the idol of self-preservation.

Just as Jesus longed for the disciples to avert their gaze from the worldly temple, He longs for us to stop worrying about building our own life and begin resting in His love.

The widow's gift was biggest of all because it came from a resting heart that trusted God. Jesus knew she gratefully gave all she had. Big trusting hearts are cultivated in quiet rest in His arms of love.

A great shaking has begun. When we stop and get honest with ourselves we can observe and feel a haunting dread and increasing anxiety in the world. All creation is groaning. The tsunamis, earthquakes, and floods are increasing as a natural sign of the deeper spiritual shaking. World markets are unstable. More followers of Christ have been martyred in the last twenty years than in the previous two thousand years.

The Lord Jesus is not worried. He said these things would come. The truth is that God's mercy is now raining down over all humanity, flooding the earth with real love. God's judgment is falling hard upon the Devil and the raging forces of darkness. This is a wonderful time to be alive! This is not doomsday; this is God's day!

The shaking will become so great that only those resting in Jesus will not lose heart. The shaking will drive many broken people into the arms of Jesus. We must be ready to receive them with open arms—from a position of intimacy in Him. It's cookie time!

Let's begin the "receiving" now and rest ourselves in His embrace of grace. Let us lay down our lives as we speak tenderly to the whole earth, "Come rest in His love!"

Secure in His arms, you can begin cultivating a resting heart by turning away from your fears.

Secure in His arms, you can begin talking to Him through honest prayer.

Secure in His arms, you can begin tuning into His voice by reading His Scripture.

Secure in His arms, you can let go of trying to run your life in this big troubled world.

COME REST

Secure in His arms, you can let Him grow your heart big with childlike trust.

Psalm 131 is one of the shortest psalms. Memorize your favorite version and pray it aloud often. Stop striving in your own strength and start cultivating His love.

God, I'm not trying to rule the roost,
I don't want to be king of the mountain.
I haven't meddled where I have no business
or fantasized grandiose plans.
I've kept my feet on the ground,
I've cultivated a quiet heart.
Like a baby content in its mother's arms,
my soul is a baby content.
Wait, Israel, for God. Wait with hope.
Hope now, hope always! (Psalm 131, MSG)

CHAPTER 2

OPEN ARMS

Come to Me... Take My yoke... learn from Me...
and you will find rest...
> — *Matthew 11:28–29, NKJV*

Brother Lawrence lived in the 1600s and "practiced the presence of God" for several decades while he washed dishes in a monastery.[1] He came to see life as a simple, wholehearted friendship with Jesus. Then he arrived at a turning point in his relationship with the Lord.

One day he was lovingly convicted by the Lord of some sin but did not feel the condemnation and self-loathing that had normally accompanied his repentance. He realized that his friend Jesus had taken him to a new level of a love relationship. Rather than feeling shameful and heavy-hearted, he simply exclaimed, "Master, look at me. The moment I turn away from your face, I stumble!" For the rest of his life, his relationship with the Lord was marked by fruitful intimacy, some stumbling,

---

1   Brother Lawrence, *The Practice of the Presence of God* (The Treasury of Christian Spiritual Classics, Thomas Nelson Publishers, 1994).

and consequent gentleness and confidence in repentance. Condemnation was replaced by companionship.

Brother Lawrence, laboring with and loving Jesus in a kitchen of obscurity, became the most sought-after spiritual counsel in all of Western Europe. The same Holy Spirit who called to Brother Lawrence is calling to us today. Amazing things happen when we get in the habit of letting Jesus love us and lead us. The moment we turn away from His face, He calls to us in loving conviction, "Turn back to me."

Several years ago, I first read of this in his little book, *The Practice of the Presence of God.* Since that time I have had a recurring picture in my mind of Jesus opening His arms to us, never pointing His finger. You will see my use of this image several times in this book.

Declaring the offer of Jesus' open arms to individuals and groups can cut through any darkness. It communicates His loving heart as He gave the great invitation in Matthew 11:28: "Come to Me, all you who labor and are heavy laden, and I will give you rest" (NKJV). It is the same image that comes to mind every time I invite someone to rest in His love.

Notice that the Holy Spirit placed Matthew 11 before Matthew 22, which is before Matthew 28. No one can hope to fulfill the great commandment of Matthew 22 (total worship of Jesus) or the great commission of Matthew 28 (total evangelism for Jesus) until they have truly accepted the great invitation of Matthew 11 (total surrender to Jesus).

You can't love the Lord and others with all your heart until you learn to let the Lord love you daily with all His heart. He is such a gentle teacher. Be loved. Be teachable.

CHAPTER 3

THE JEDIDIAH IDENTITY

Then David comforted Bathsheba, his wife, and slept with her. She became pregnant and gave birth to a son, and they named him Solomon. The Lord loved the child and sent word through Nathan the prophet that they should name him Jedidiah (which means "beloved of the Lord") as the Lord had commanded.

— 2 Samuel 12:24–25

What defines you? Is it *what you do?* Some find their meaning in life by "making a difference." But what happens when you don't? Fear of failure can become your god when you find your identity through making a difference.

What defines you? Is it *who you are?* Some think they have found enlightenment in the saying, "It's not what you do but who you are that matters." Unfortunately, that thinking sets us up for a self-centered life—"I"dolatry. Fortunately, there is another way.

The Bible tells the famous story of David and Bathsheba. King David, a man who loved God with all his heart, made horrible choices in arranging the death of Bathsheba's husband (Uriah, his loyal friend and soldier) so he could take Bathsheba as his own. God confronted him through the prophet Nathan,

27

and David repented. (Sometime read David's prayer of repentance in Psalm 51. If you ever blow it, pray that prayer with all your heart and watch what happens.)

Though God forgave him, David experienced the painful consequences of his choices.

After the death of the child conceived in his adulterous affair with Bathsheba, David took her in as one of his wives. They named their next child Solomon, which means "peaceable." They were declaring, "We've been through a lot, but maybe we can have some peace now." They were like many people in our day, hoping for mere survival and maybe a little peace. It's the best the world hopes for, and the best the world can offer.

But Jesus offers so much more.

Notice that "*they* named him Solomon," but the *Lord* named him *Jedidiah*—"beloved of the Lord."

As long as Solomon found his identity in *being loved* by the Lord, he became the wise king. But when he found his identity in being the wise king, he was given over to idolatry. Each one who is saved in Christ is His "Jedidiah." This identity is the Lord's desire for every person. When you find your identity in what you do, your security depends upon your performance; but when you find your identity in *being loved by the Lord*, your security depends upon *His* performance.

We often make statements like, "I am a pastor... I am a teacher... I am a mother... I am a consultant... I am a student... I am an athlete"—often statements of identity. The truth is not that *I am* a pastor, but that *I am* a beloved child of the Lord who is doing the work of pastor.

If my happiness depends on what happens, the evil one can steal my happiness away. But if I rest in being the Lord's beloved, then real *life* begins to well up inside me to overflowing.

LETTING JESUS LOVE YOU

Jesus says, "The thief does not come except to steal, and to kill, and to destroy. I have come that they may have life, and that they may have *it* more abundantly" (John 10:10, NKJV).

When my daughter Emily was editor of her college newspaper, she wrote an opinion column entitled, "Avoid identity theft, just be a schmuck!" Nice satire! Who wants to steal your identity if it's not worth anything? However, the Bible says you were made in God's image; you are of ultimate value to Him.

"This is real love. It is not that we loved God, but that he loved us and sent his Son as a sacrifice to take away our sins" (1 John 4:10). Out of his *real* love for you, God sent His Son to *rescue* you by dying on the cross for you. The Lord invites you to come to Him and find real rest, real love, and the real identity He has won for you—the Jedidiah identity.

What's in a name? As a Jedidiah, you would let more and more of Jesus' loving presence rest upon you, and as you let Him be enough for you, He will transform your life.

Make no mistake, there is an enemy who wants not only to steal your identity but to kill and utterly destroy you. However, the One who made you *loves you*. This wonderful rescuer, Jesus, died on a cross for all of us schmucks! He wants to rescue and fill you with life overflowing. Let Him. He wants to reveal to you the secret of true contentment: let it be enough to just be loved by Him.

COME REST

LET'S PRAY!

Lord, You know how driven I can be. I'm so tired of proving my own worth. It's lonely being so dependent on myself. I need more than just a little peace. I'm tired of finding my identity in what I do. I want to enjoy life as Your beloved child. I sometimes act as if You are not there and don't care about me. Please forgive me. Help me feel secure in Your love. I choose to let You love me. Please show me how much You love me. Teach me to let Your love be enough. Shine Your light on the dark stuff in me. I give my hurts, fears, and angers to You. Clean me out! Fill me up with Your love.

I am putting my life truly in Your hands. My security now depends upon Your performance, not mine. I am Your Jedidiah.

In Jesus' name, amen.

CHAPTER 4

WEEDS AND WONDER

He lets me rest in green meadows… — *Psalm 23:2*

When Kim and I were first married, we'd be driving down the highway and she would cry, "Look, look, how gorgeous, the Queen Anne's Lace and the blue Chicory!" I would shout, "Where, where?" All I could see were weeds in the ditches.

Kim would give me that look that said, "Come on, city boy, time for another lesson!" So one time I pulled over onto the shoulder and we got out, with Kim bounding into the ditch and me trailing tentatively behind.

She said, "My daddy would often come home to my mom with a bouquet of these, just because he loved her!"

I was thinking, *"A fistful of weeds?"*

Knowingly, she picked some, held them close to me, and began pointing out the beautiful intricacy of each flower. Flower? Did I say flower? Yes, suddenly my "blind eyes" were opened to see the weeds transformed before my eyes. How beautiful!

COME REST

How driven I had always been while driving highways! But tunnel vision no more! The Lord has certainly used Kim all these years to open my eyes wide in wonder at His loving care expressed in His creation!

And if God cares so wonderfully for wildflowers that are here today and thrown into the fire tomorrow, he will certainly care for you (Matt. 6:30).

Ever since that first encounter in the ditch, I have been hungry to feast my eyes on the Lord's beauty in creation. You too can do what Jesus says and look closely at the lilies of the field. See more deeply the tender loving care God has for all of us in creation. Of course, we are not to worship creation, but we certainly are to worship the Creator. As my old friends from the now-defunct music group "Three Crosses" used to sing, "God painted better than Michelangelo!"

I remember the day I hugged a big tree. I felt its breadth and groundedness. Yes, you heard me! That's why Jesus encourages us in Matthew 6 to go out and enjoy birds and flowers. If you rest from drivenness and tunnel vision—if you let birds be birds and weeds become flowers—you can begin to let God be God, a God who lets you simply be you. Soon you will realize He made all this beauty because He loves beauty…and because He loves you. Look closely and let Him open your eyes wide in wonder at His love.

Come, my love, let us go out to the fields and spend the night among the wildflowers (Song of Sol. 7:11).

LETTING JESUS LOVE YOU

One year, on our anniversary, I gave thanks to the Lord for Kim, who I sometimes call Bright Eyes, by composing a simple verse:

As a boy,
I felt destined for politics and riches
But through Bright Eyes I found glory
In weeds in the ditches!

CHAPTER 5

LOVE COVERS

Most important of all, continue to show deep love for each other, for love covers a multitude of sins.

— *1 Peter 4:8*

I do not have much artistic or mechanical ability. But I do have a lovely mechanical pen with beautiful African wood grain—and I made it! Well, I did have a "little" help.

Kim and I once went to a wonderful pastors' retreat in Wisconsin. In the midst of a week of deep spiritual searching, I accepted the retreat director's offer for a little recreation. He would teach me how to make a pen in his woodworking shop. His name was Andy, a gentle man of prayer with twinkling eyes.

I chose my own wood cartridges—hollowed out blocks which would eventually house the inner mechanism. I picked a little block of deep, dark wood and another block of rich, red wood. Andy showed me how to place the blocks on the wood lathe and turn it on. He then produced what he described as "an expensive knife" with a sharp, beveled blade. He demonstrated how to keep the knife "firm yet relaxed" as he gently passed the knife across the rapidly spinning wood. He cautioned me to not push or jerk the knife as it would destroy both the wood and the knife. Great! Thanks, Andy! That helped me relax!

I flipped the switch and heard the high-pitched whir of the spinning lathe. I nervously took the knife in my hands and ever-so-slightly applied the tip of the knife to the spinning wood blocks. I tried so hard to keep the knife perfectly steady. However, the harder I tried the more gouges and grooves I created.

Andy asked, "How's it going?" He already knew the answer, yet he said, "You're doing well." I thought, *Yeah, right, I'm shredding it!*

"Let me show you something," Andy gently said. I reluctantly, yet gratefully, turned the knife over to him. He said, "You're holding too tight onto the knife. Remember, firm but relaxed."

As I watched I realized that he was letting the knife move in concert with the spinning wood. He was focused on keeping the knife moving in a gentle, firm manner. I had been fixated on the particular point of contact right in front of the knife. It reminded me of golf; hackers hit at the ball, but true golfers swing through the ball. Something clicked. *Stop fixating and let it flow.*

I watched as his gentle, confident strokes completely smoothed over my awkward gashes and grooves.

I took hold of the knife to try again and moved a little more freely across the spinning wood, though occasionally still pressing and gouging. Once more, Andy said, "Much better…let me have a go." As I stood back I could still see much unevenness, and we were getting near the end of the project. After all, a wood block is not inexhaustible. You can only tool it to a certain thickness before cracking or punching through it. I was so relieved for Andy to smooth it out. Then he added a customized fluting to one of the blocks. Wow!

Andy then gave me a choice of varnish or mild rubbing compound. I chose the compound for a more natural finish. The last phase was applying light sandpaper, with light pressure to smooth the finish. Then came the insertion of the mechanical parts from the kit.

As I admired my new creation, it hit me. I said, "Andy, this is my *Love Covers* pen!" He said, "What do you mean?" I replied, "The Scriptures say love covers a multitude of sins." I held the pen toward him and said, "You smoothed over my gouges!"

We both laughed, rejoicing that Jesus' loving death covers our sin. My pen is a constant reminder. Life is short, subject to much striving, fretting, and gouging. I make many choices and efforts to live right—but only Jesus, His blood, and His love can make something beautiful of my life.

We fail Him, but He does not fail us. His love covers a multitude of our sins. It's important to remember that when we fall short of pleasing each other. Will we let His love be enough for us? Or will we fixate on the specific point of failure, hurt, and offense? Will we let go and let His love flow through us toward each other and into a nervous world?

Gratitude to Jesus is at the heart of deep love for others. The next time your child, parent, spouse, friend, or enemy fails or hurts you, turn your hurting heart away from focusing on their offense and look upon Him, declaring "Love Covers!"

CHAPTER 6

THE FINAL DISTANCE

Come to me...

In the movie *Hitch*, Will Smith plays a "date doctor" named Hitch who gives men counsel on how to begin a sensitive relationship with a woman. (The movie is a good picture of how the secular world views male-female relationships). The date doctor knows all the right moves but has a broken, rejected, clumsy heart beneath his suave manner. His relationship coaching is actually a way for him to hide from resolution of his past broken relationships. Actor Kevin James plays a hapless accountant named Arnold who is "way out of his league" in love with a celebrity. Hitch loves Arnold's enthusiasm and accepts the challenge to help him win her heart. There is a hilarious scene in which Hitch leads Arnold in a role playing session rehearsing for a first kiss. Hitch tells Arnold that when it's time, the man must go 90 percent of the distance toward the woman and then wait for the woman to come to him the remaining 10 percent. Then he will know if the woman really wants to kiss him.

In the movie, this 90/10 principle is couched in fear of rejection and manipulation. However, it has one undeniable connection to Jesus' great invitation. The Lord does not grab us and force us to relate to Him. He does not coerce, manipulate, or deny our will. But He does come near, inviting us, waiting for us to come to Him. The choice to come the final distance is ours. He wants us, has cleared away every obstacle between us, and waits to see if we want Him.

He is not a date doctor; He is the Great Physician, the lover of our souls. He is not looking for a date, a quickie, or even a meaningful relationship according to Dr. Phil! He wants you and me—forever. He has already gone through hell for you. Will you walk through your fears and doubts to Him? That's really the question, isn't it?

Jesus says, "Come to me." Responding to that invitation means leaving where I am and going to where He is. Yes, He has made the first move by dying for me, being raised for me, and coming to where I am through the Holy Spirit. Yes, I can only love Him back because He has first loved me. However, the next move is mine... and yours.

When Jesus said, "Come to Me, all you who labor and are heavy laden," He was addressing people who were weary from trying to make their own way through life. To make matters worse, religious leaders were heaping heavy rules upon people as a horrible substitute for the loving relationship God offers. There was then—and still is—so much human striving in the church. Jesus wanted us to know that His way is easy. His burden is light. True Christianity is not a heavy religion with rules but a refreshing, right relationship with Jesus!

He still comes near and waits for you to travel the final distance... of *your* fear, *your* doubts. It's a road only you can travel. It's popular to say that many roads lead to God (meaning many different religions or personal philosophies). But Jesus said, He is the narrow way that leads to life everlasting! Yet, we each have our own road to travel *to* Him. We each have our own burdens to bring to His strong arms. We each have our own wounds, fears, and doubts. What are yours?

What does it mean to come to Him? It means choosing to leave the place of our own faltering self-sufficiency and surrendering ourselves to Him. It means choosing to empty our burdens into His hands so we are free to embrace Him and be embraced. He is God and we are not. He can embrace us even as He is carrying our burdens. But we cannot embrace Him unless our arms are empty.

What keeps us from coming to Him with our burdens? First, habit, then wounds, then fear, and then doubt. We are used to carrying the load, coping with our brokenness the best we can and, though weary, we are comfortably miserable where we are. We don't want to change our position because we fear that we will end up in worse shape. We fear something worse because we doubt there is anyone who can make things better.

That's what is so wonderful about Jesus. He knows we will not come to Him until we decide we can't carry our load any more. So He waits, woos, pleads, prays, and knocks constantly *for us.* For *our sake,* He neither slumbers nor sleeps. He knows our difficulty with trust. That is exactly why He says, "Come to me." He honors our right to choose. He knows trust is a choice. No one can make the decision for us. We get to decide. The moment we decide to take the first step toward Him, we will experience freedom, healing, and rebirth. Before that moment, we are held hostage. After that moment, we never again need to be held by *anything* but Him.

I once had a conversation at a hospital with my dear cousin Kathy as my mother lay struggling with cancer in intensive care. She said, "I don't have the peace my aunt has. How do I get that peace? Do you think I could ever have that?"

Such questions are always a joyful thing because they mean the person asking is being wooed by the Lord and is very close to surrendering to Him. The Lord showed me a picture. I saw a partition between her and the Lord—the kind you find in cubicles in a large office space. The wall was not tall (she could peek over it on tiptoe) and not thick—but a barrier, nonetheless. The partition symbolized an unwillingness to trust *anyone*. I shared this with her and she immediately agreed, knowing deep inside that this was a barrier in her life. I told her that the Lord understood; He knew that her trust had been betrayed many times in life (but never by Him). He was not pointing a finger at her, just opening His arms. She agreed.

I asked her if she had ever let Jesus in to be her Lord and Savior. She said no. I begged her to let Him in. I asked her if she wanted to, and she asked me, "If I give Him control, will I be a mouse?" This was very revealing, not just about my friend, but about humanity!

Before we surrender to the Lord, we can only see our weakness as looming defeat. After we surrender to Him, we can see our weakness fading into His strong victory.

I answered her, "Am I a mouse? If you let the Lord in, He will live inside you and make you stronger than your wildest dreams. He will be your strength. You get to be *you,* with Him inside. You will be strong after the manner of Deborah, a warrior woman of God in the Bible. The Lord will pour out much compassion and wisdom upon people from now on for your whole life. It will be amazing!"

She asked, "Is this something I have to do with anyone else around?" I replied, "No one except Jesus." She said, "I think I want to let Him in." At that moment I had to let go and rest in His searching love for her. What a concept! I said, "Whenever you let Him in, let me know, and I will help you with your next step." We hugged and parted.

The next night at the hospital, her eyes twinkled as she told me, "I let Him in!" We hugged, and I gave her my Bible, asking her to read the gospel of John slowly, opening her heart to each story as she began her friendship with Jesus. She said, "I do have some peace! But when I let Him in, I didn't feel anything. Is that right?" I told her that when we receive Jesus by faith, we don't necessarily feel anything. But then I directed her to Luke 11, in which Jesus tells us to constantly ask for the Holy Spirit. I promised her that if she keeps asking for Jesus to fill her with the Holy Spirit, sooner or later she will feel Him filling her with His love and power! How true, if we keep asking. Again, He wants to know how much we want all of Him.

The beautiful thing about letting Jesus love you and lead you is that you don't lose your true identity, you gain it. You become His beloved, His Jedidiah, *and* you get to be you— the you that He made you to be. Slowly and surely, He will show you that being loved by Him is more than enough, as the world's glitter fades in the fire of His loving heart. More and more, your heart will gratefully burst forth with the fire of His love for everyone around you.

The truth is, even after we surrender to Jesus the very first time, life can be rough. We will need to turn and come to Jesus many times after the first time. Being His disciple means living a life of continual surrender. Every time we do, no matter how we have stumbled, He always takes us even deeper into His heart than ever before. You see, coming that first "final distance" is just the beginning of Him leading you on a wonderful adventure to your final destination.

A year after that first conversation, just before my cousin's mother died, we talked again. She had continued to journey with the Lord and had recently cried out in angry despair to the Lord about her mama. Suddenly, for the first time in her life, she felt a tangible warm presence on her shoulder—like a hand. She knew instantly nobody was there—except the Lord! We prayed together as she asked for more of the Holy Spirit to keep filling her to overflowing. The Lord is faithful, and loves us so.

CHAPTER 7

SWEET OBSESSION

The Lord is not slack concerning His promise, as some count slackness, but is longsuffering toward us, not willing that any should perish but that all should come to repentance.

— 2 Peter 3:9, NKJV

It became a ritual of love, longing, and celebration. We experienced it from two perspectives—the eyes of my sixteen-month-old son Daniel... and the eyes of the man trying so hard to be his faithful father and a faithful pastor. We shared breakfast followed by morning hugs and kisses. As I drove away to work I knew I could count on a "last goodbye" act.

The moment I went to my car, Daniel would run to the front room, climb onto the heat register under the picture window, and wriggle between the drapes to watch me drive away. He kept waving until I was out of sight. He would continue to look out for a while before returning to all the day's activities with his mama and big sister, Emily.

When it was time for me to return for supper, his ears would perk up at any sound that might be me. When he heard my car door slam in the garage, he knew for sure! He would look up, gasp, shriek with delightful anticipation, and begin shouting the declaration that still rings in my heart eighteen years later.

You see, as a young, overworked, overachieving senior pastor, I approached the back steps to the kitchen door in a mental fog, not yet disengaged from thoughts of work. Ever been there?

Suddenly, the sweet music of my toddler's joyful cries dissolved my fatigue. His words are forever emblazoned on my heart, "Dadu's home, Dadu's home, Dadu's home!" It did not matter what I held in my arms—I had to empty them because Dadu was home, and my son was running with dead aim at my embrace. It was an embrace of grace for both of us. The longing was over, and the celebration of each other was on!

The Lord granted me such sweetness with my son simply because He loves me and wanted to give me a taste of what He desires for me: daily delight in each precious day until He returns, followed by eternal delight beginning the instant my spirit hears the last trumpet at His return. This delight and longing, this sweet obsession, has always typified true Christianity. I am at my best when I daily expect to see the return of the Lord in my lifetime.

There are advancing signals the time is growing short. If we are honest, the accelerating anxiety, violence, immorality, idolatry, demonic rage, and divine judgments all hauntingly remind us that this old world is near its end.

But joyfully, the welling up of faith, hope, and love in the hearts of Jesus' followers worldwide, accompanied by signs and wonders, signals the kingdom of our God is on the move. His new world of heaven on earth is mercifully near.

In a tender prayer time, a dear prayer warrior friend, Vi Ahomana shared this deep insight from the Lord; Jesus longs to return to the world He died for. He longs for us more than we know. He hurts so much for us and it's as if He is asking the Father if He can go now. But the Father says, "Not yet, Son."

The evil one would have us believe the lie that Jesus doesn't care, isn't there, and is not coming back to set things right. But consider this piercing truth from 2 Peter 3:9: "The Lord is not slack concerning *His* promise, as some count slackness, but is longsuffering toward us, not willing that any should perish but that all should come to repentance." What a loving, longsuffering Lord we have!

He is not obsessed with His return, but ours.

As you read this, it's still not too late. Return before He does. Let go of all the lies, doubts, and fears. Open your arms, run to Him, and cry "Dadu's home!" Before you know it, He will be. Delight in His embrace of grace.

CHAPTER 8

DROWNING?

For the Son of Man came to seek and save those who are lost.
— *Luke 19:10*

When I was about twelve years old, my family joined some other families at a lake for the day. I wasn't a very good swimmer but I wanted to prove to my older friend that I could make it across the lake. I swam out past the deep ropes but tired and stalled in really deep water. I tried bouncing up from the bottom, only to sink back in over my head. I began to panic. My friend went to get his dad. I kept bouncing, gasping for air on each bounce. But the more I bounced the farther into the deep I went. My arms and legs felt so heavy, the pressure on my chest increased. I kept trying to spit out any water coming into my mouth. The harder I worked the more powerless I became. Have you ever felt like that?

After what seemed like forever, I saw my friend's father paddling fast in my direction on his air mattress, leading a train of other friends paddling on their mattresses. As he arrived, he reached for me and I weakly struggled to take hold of his hand. I then felt his hand take hold of my lower arm, and he lifted me up. I was rescued.

Every time I think of that day, I think of what Jesus has done for me. His mission is simple: to rescue me—and you. I was once drowning in sin and fear, and He died on a cross to rescue me. Why would He do that?

John 3:16 says, "For God loved the world so much that he gave his one and only Son, so that everyone who believes in him will not perish but have eternal life." The word *believe* in the New Testament means "to take hold of." When you first truly believe in Jesus, taking hold of His outstretched hand, He promises to never let you go...because He loves you.

John 10:28 says, "I give them eternal life, and they will never perish. No one can snatch them away from me." When my friend's father reached into the water and gripped my lower arm, I felt relieved and took hold, then he took me to safety. As we proceeded, my grip weakened and my fear would return for a moment. But his grip held firm, and I knew I was rescued *and* safe.

Jesus loves you. Jesus wants a relationship with you. Jesus wants you to take hold. Once you do, He will never let go. In fact, if you let Him, He will lead you in a never-ending, upward cycle:

He loves me and reaches out to save me

I take hold

He takes me closer to His heart

I weaken and slip

He grips me

I take hold again

He lifts me up and takes me

Closer to His heart, over and over,

Higher and higher, deeper and deeper.

COME REST

I first took hold of Jesus as a small child, praying to Him at bedtime with my Jesus-loving parents close by. As a pre-teen, Jesus reached out to me again through a pastor's sermon during my confirmation preparation. The preacher pleaded with everyone to "ask Jesus to come into your heart, forgive your sins, and be your Savior and Lord." That's exactly what I did.

Then came high school. I was trying hard with my own willpower to be a good Christian, rather than relying on Jesus. People thought I was "a fine young man." But I knew there were parts of my life that were not as the Lord wanted. I struggled with lust and didn't feel like I could talk to anybody about it. And I was constantly frustrated because I wanted athletic success and fame but had a minor problem—I didn't have enough talent! The thought that I should pray often came into my mind and, funny thing, when I did, things got better. Who gave me those thoughts to pray?

In college, I was engaged to be married, but we broke up and I was devastated. I tried to drown my sorrows with beer and women. Can you believe that I once danced in the discos of the seventies for five hours at a pop in shoes with four-inch platforms? I was searching for love in all the wrong places. But I remember the night I sat straight up in bed and knew deep in my heart that I had to stop what I was doing. Guess who was giving that deep feeling? He never lets go! I went to my pastor, and he encouraged me. Eventually, I started helping with the youth group.

Then came law school. I wanted to change the world through politics, but I ran straight into academic failure for the first time in my life. I flunked one course, and soon I was back drowning my sorrows in the discos. It was like I had an angel on one shoulder and a devil on the other. Looking back, I'm sure that was the case.

LETTING JESUS LOVE YOU

Finally, I came to the end of myself. I knew law school was not for me. My heart was just not in it. I was tired of living a double-minded life. And I kept having the most embarrassing thought, over and over again: *I was supposed to be a pastor.* Finally, I couldn't stand it. With my heart pounding, I said to my pastor, Gene Miller, "I've been thinking I'm supposed to become a minister, but I know I'm not holy enough."

He looked at me with eyes of kindness and said, "Well I'm sure there are some adjustments the Lord wants you to make. But you are a real person with real gifts that can help real people with their problems, and the Lord wants people like you to lead His church." I couldn't believe it. I felt so loved in a way I did not deserve. Jesus wanted me. He knew everything about me and loved me anyway. And He wanted to use me to bless others. What a love! What a Jesus! This time, when He reached out I took hold and never looked back.

Though I have sometimes slipped into doubt, worry, or ambition in these last twenty-nine years, Jesus has been so faithful and generous to me. He has shown me how to rest in Him for victory over lust and worry. He has blessed me with a wonderful wife and twenty-eight years of a faithful, happy marriage; He gave us two children who are saved, love Jesus back, and are just plain enjoyable. He has also blessed me with a fruitful ministry and the privilege of telling *you* that...

Jesus likes you.

Jesus loves you.

Jesus wants you to *take hold.*

Maybe you have heard someone say "I love Jesus!" But you honestly don't. You might like to love Jesus, but you can't say that you feel that right now. That's OK. If you have never really taken hold of Jesus, it's impossible to feel that way about Him. Give yourself a break. Why can I say this? Because 1 John 4:19 says, "We love each other because he loved us first."

Come Rest

I'm not really capable of loving Jesus or anyone else until I let Jesus love me first, taking hold of His arms of love. You don't have to love Him right now. Just let go and say yes to Him. John 1:12 says, "But to all who believed him and accepted him, he gave the right to become children of God." The moment you take hold of Jesus and really mean it, He comes into your heart and you are born brand new as a true child of God. He rescues you. He saves you. And you get to grow as a baby Christian, starting from right where you are. Jesus will fill you with His love and you'll start feeling more love for Him. And guess what else will happen?

You will no longer have to worry about what will happen to you on Judgment Day. John 3:18 says, "There is no judgment against anyone who believes in him." You belong to Jesus, and He is your free ticket into heaven. Everyone who takes hold of Jesus gets taken to heaven with Him. Isn't that awesome?

And that's all because of Him! It's because He made the first move. Why? He loves you. "This is real love—not that we loved God, but that he loved us and sent his Son as a sacrifice to take away our sins" (1 John 4:10).

As you read this, there is only one perfect person in the room and it's not you. Yes, it's Jesus. Ever since He saved me, He has been a much better leader than I have been a follower. He doesn't expect us to be perfect because He is. He is saying to you, "Just let me love you and lead you—I'll take care of everything else." Are you tired of trying to keep your head above water? A strong hand is reaching out to you. Take hold!

Let's Pray:

Lord, I am a mixture of many thoughts and feelings. I hate to admit it, but I am weak. Yet I'm glad to admit that I need You. Thank You for reaching out to me. I now reach out to take hold of Your hand. Lift me up. I am Yours. You are mine. Amen.

CHAPTER 9

BACK TO FIRST LOVE

No man can serve two masters...

— *Matt. 6:24*

My sheep hear My voice...

— *John 10:27, NKJV*

My path to writing this book took a major turn twenty years ago...

"You've broken through. You are on your way. It's all laid out for you. You are going to be a bishop one day; you will be pastoring the largest churches in the land. You have done very well." These were voices in my ear, some coming to me from older, cynical pastor friends, some coming from within. I had just received the first round of congratulations from friends after hearing the news that I was now the youngest man anyone could remember being assigned to pastor such a large church in our state.

As I shared these comments with my wife, Kim, I saw her look of loving concern. She said, "I don't like what these people are saying to you, it's not right. I don't like what all this political talk does to you. It's not right."

Come Rest

"I know," I replied. Deep inside, I knew she was right. We pulled up to a movie rental store and I left Kim to watch over our small children. She prayed. In the time it took for me to rent a movie, something happened in Kim that proved to be a crossroads in our life.

When I got back in the car, she said, "The Lord just wrote a song in me for you." Her eyes had that joyful, teary, loving look that wins me over, and over again. I said, "Please sing it to me." In her tender second-soprano voice, I heard these words:

There are two voices in every ear
Two voices we all can hear,
Two voices in every ear,
Will you choose the voice of your God?

There's the voice of God
And the voice of the world.
A call to service,
A lure to success
One way only can set you free,
Will you choose the voice of your God?

There are two voices in every ear
Two voices we all can hear,
Two voices in every ear,
Will you choose the voice of your God?

We held each other and cried. I rested in arms of grace—Kim's and the Lord's. I was known, loved, and called. For that crucial moment, the siren song of the "lure to success" was drowned out.

I had been shopping movies to "escape," while the Lord was showing me the way out of the snare of over-achieving compulsions. He had spoken powerfully to me through Kim.

From then on, I knew I must listen more intently, and *only,* to *His* "call of service." I had a long way to go, but a loving, knowing Lord to lead me...

...Back To First Love

Weary and burdened by my own expectations of myself, I signed up for a week of retreat for the first time in my life. I would join thirty other pastors to learn and practice several historic spiritual disciplines. We gathered in the spring of 1988 at a convent on the campus of Mount Mercy College in Cedar Rapids, Iowa. I had only been to that city once before. I did not know I was about to come "home."

Having read Richard Foster's *Celebration of Discipline* and Thomas Merton's *New Seeds of Contemplation* in the previous two years, I had begun attempting disciplined prayer. First attempts to rest in Him through prayer proved to be a fitful wrestling with silence—facing my fears of aloneness. Drawing apart, I had found haven in the structure and resources provided by Rueben Job's *A Guide to Prayer for Ministers and Other Servants.*

Yet, getting away for an entire week to practice opening up to the Spirit raised the questions, "Is there a Spirit to open up to? Are these mere exercises or real encounter?" I arrived thirsty, yet already lonely for my dear wife and small children.

Early in the week, we were asked to go back to our individual rooms for prayer and meditation. We were specifically instructed to sit upright in a straight chair, close our eyes, and open our hearts to Jesus. We were to envision an outdoor scene that was a place of peace. Then we were to invite Jesus to come meet us in that place and to let Him speak and lead.

I sat down, closed my eyes, began to breathe easily, and asked the Lord to bring into my mind a peaceful meeting place. Simply and suddenly, I saw a large flat rock overlooking a bubbling stream, with a meadow and surrounding forest in the background. The sky was deep blue. I looked around and then came back to focus on the rock.

I asked Jesus to meet with me. I saw Him first at a distance as He made His way to the rock. He sat down and looked to me with smiling eyes. I chose to walk to Him and sat down beside Him as He opened His arms. I laid my head on His chest, listening to His heartbeat, and let Him hold me…and I rested. I was so tired…of all the expectations…of everything. I let Him hold me for what seemed like ninety whole seconds.

When I opened my eyes and looked at the clock on my desk, it was forty-five whole *minutes* later. I had *not* been sleeping. In that moment I knew He had come to me, not as a figment of my imagination but as the One to whom I was introduced as a small child by my parents and grandmother. I had come back to my First Love. I was free, once again, to trust and rest in His love.

THE GREAT INVITATION

Fast-forwarding to just five years ago…I asked the Lord to give me a "life message"—a focused mission through which He would minister to people for the rest of my life. In an unfolding process of Scripture, prayer, counsel, and trial and error, I heard Him say to my heart, "Tell the earth, 'Come Rest in My Love.' "

His invitation is based on Matthew 11:28–30 and Revelation 2:1–8. In Matthew, Jesus sums up the fundamental need of humanity in one word—rest. In Revelation, Jesus offers the only path to real rest—intimacy with Him as our First Love.

St. Augustine once said, "Great art thou, O Lord... for Thou hast made us for Thyself, and our heart is restless until it finds its repose in thee."[1] Real rest is not temporary respite or retreat (as healthy as they may be). Real rest is certainly not resignation or withdrawal (as unhealthy as they may be). It is not absence of stress, but the presence of the Lord. It is not found in fighting to have moments for yourself but in surrendering moment by moment to Jesus. Rest is not passive but is the most aggressive way to make a difference in this world. You can't make your mark until you stop trying, because your life can't yield real fruit until you yield to Him.

After thirty years of ministry I have learned that every human buckles under the pressure of trying to run their own life. It doesn't work. We harm ourselves and others. You have a choice—run yourself into the ground or let Him run your life on solid ground. Jesus knows that real rest is something only He can give. The end of your striving will be the beginning of His thriving—when you rest in Him, His love becomes real to you, in you, and through you.

A dear friend, teacher, and "the messenger of Christlikeness," Francis Frangipane has told me, "When God gives a man a message for others, He is telling him a lot about what He is going to do with him!"

When I first received this mandate to spread the Lord's invitation to come rest, I thought I knew what it meant to rest in the Lord. I now realize I didn't have a clue! Once I received His mandate, the Lord immediately took me through three years of "fire"—testing in resting! In the process, He moved

---

1   St. Augustine, *The Confessions of St. Augustine* (The Treasury of Christian Spiritual Classics, Nashville, TN: Thomas Nelson Publishers 1994), p.11.

to burn the fear of man out of me and replace it with fear of the Lord and love for man. I heard the Lord say to my heart, "How low will you go for Me?"

After encountering severe challenges, the Lord brought me to a place where I realized that the heart of resting in Him is... trust. He is constantly faithful and we can constantly trust Him! Real rest is real trust.

If I keep giving control of my life over to Jesus, He *will* lead me in all my flaws and circumstances and fill me with overflowing love—no matter what. However, if I choose to stay in control, or give control to any other person or philosophy, my life can end in emptiness and destruction. In this complicated world, it's that simple.

Are you sick and tired of being sick and tired? Are you restless to be rid of restlessness? The end of your striving will be the beginning of His thriving! Come rest in His love.

CHAPTER 10

STILL

Be still, and know that I am God!

— *Psalm 46:10*

It was a perfect sun-splashed June afternoon. We took our eighteen-month-old daughter, Emily, to the park for picnic fun. After lunch, we sat back and let Emily explore—in our plain view. She delighted in the relative freedom of wandering in the midst of both yellow and puff ball dandelions about thirty yards away from our picnic table.

Emily stepped just a little farther, losing all awareness of her position. Our eyes never left her. She made her way in the direction of the tennis courts. We thought, "That's about far enough."

Suddenly, a large groundskeeper mower fired up and completely drowned out the serenity of the small park. Emily was startled and looked about, but she could not locate us. She began crying, as I ran toward her and shouted her name. She could not hear my voice through the mower noise and all her sobbing. She was safe, but didn't know it. She turned and saw me just before I scooped her up in my arms. She held on so tight.

When you are hurting or afraid, it's good to cry out to the Lord for help. He promises He will draw near to you as you draw near to Him. He runs to you. Yet, if you have been hurting and crying out a long time, but don't feel His presence and still don't hear His voice, try this: be still.

Choose to rest from crying out, speaking, thinking, complaining, being busy, worrying, and thrill seeking... stop... be still.

Before you know it...you will hear His voice in your heart. You will know He is with you, and you will discover that He has been calling out to you the whole time. You just couldn't hear Him because of all the noise—mostly coming from you!

However, sometimes we are simply rebellious—unwilling to live for Him. Then He is silent to our requests. In Isaiah 58, the Lord says we don't get quick replies to prayer when we live for ourselves and not for Him. It's selfish noise. He will not grant our requests when they are against His will. He waits for us to be still and yield to Him.

The next time you are so panicked that you can't hear or see God, be still... and you will hear Him saying, "I love you...still."

CHAPTER 11

HIDING SIDEWAYS

Perfect love expels all fear.

— *1 John 4:18*

Since recently beginning a new ministry, I have noticed the occasional sensation and alarm of "free-falling," struggling with loneliness, fear, and doubt.

One day a picture came into my mind. I saw me standing only one foot away from Jesus, within the loving arc of His outstretched arms, yet turned away so that my shoulders were perpendicular to His chest. So close, yet so far. Have you ever tried to hug someone while turned away from them? The Lord showed me I was "hiding sideways" from Him.

That's what was happening to many of the believers at Ephesus in the second chapter of Revelation:

I know your works, your labor, your patience, and that you cannot bear those who are evil. And you have tested those who say they are apostles and are not, and have found them liars; and you have persevered and have patience, and have labored for My name's sake and have not become weary. Nevertheless I have this against you, that you have left your first love. Remember therefore from where you have fallen; repent and do the first works, or else I will come to you quickly and remove your lampstand from its place—unless you repent. But this you have, that you hate the deeds of the Nicolaitans, which I also hate. "He who has an ear, let him hear what the Spirit says to the churches. To him who overcomes I will give to eat from the tree of life, which is in the midst of the Paradise of God" (Rev. 2:2–7, NKJV).

The believers at Ephesus were certainly standing *against* immorality and *against* false doctrine. However, the Lord had one major complaint—they were not leaning *against* Him in full intimate embrace. When there's no real intimacy with Jesus as our first love, there's no real power released in our lives.

The Holy Spirit is seeking to convict modern hearts just like the Ephesians—convict, not condemn. The Lord's desire is always to draw us into His embrace of grace. We can be standing on His truth, and standing against the lies of the evil one, yet turned away from full embrace with the Savior who first saved us.

What a paradox, the Lord mercifully died in our place for our sins, but He will not tolerate our lack of intimacy with Him. When He sees us begin to turn away, He always moves to call us back—oftentimes simply by standing by and allowing us to experience a profound sense of His absence.

Sadly, we often do not immediately turn back to Him. Instead, we turn away and encounter a flood of loneliness. We turn toward people and things we think will bring comfort, even religious acts. For example, we turn away ever so slightly and settle for singing praise songs instead of singing praise *to* Him. We say prayers rather than talking *to* Him. We may even share our pain with other believers but never cry out *to* Him. We hide from Him by doing everything spiritual except coming to Him. We hold God at arm's length by being religious instead of loving.

He can only be our First Love when we consistently go to Him with our joys, our thanks, our questions, our requests, and our complaints—FIRST! If He is not first, then all our sincere spiritual striving is the practical equivalent of atheism. He is not a theological principle to be applied, He is a Person to be loved.

Much activity in today's church is well-intentioned "fellowship" but not intimate "followship." Jesus is alive and available to us through the person and power of the Holy Spirit. Once we get in the habit of going to Him first, letting Him love us, loving Him back—then He is more than happy to lead us on our mission. First things first.

In John 15:5 Jesus says, "I am the vine, you are the branches. He who abides in Me, and I in him, bears much fruit; for without Me you can do nothing." The only way to do a true work of God is to choose to yield and draw life from the Arms of Love we initially trusted for rescue.

Abiding is continued believing, continued surrender—resting in Jesus as your First Love.

As we have seen, *believe* means to "take hold" like a drowning person does with a rescuer's outstretched hand. The word implies continual surrender. Look at Hebrews 4:3–11:

> For only we who *believe* can enter his rest... So God's rest is there for people to enter, but those who first heard this good news failed to enter because they disobeyed God. So God set another time for entering his rest, and that time is today. God announced this through David much later in the words already quoted: "Today when you hear his voice, don't harden your hearts." ...So there is a special rest still waiting for the people of God. For all who have entered into God's rest have rested from their labors, just as God did after

creating the world. So let us do our best to enter that rest. But if we disobey God, as the people of Israel did, we will fall.

Each new day, each present moment, you can choose to rest in Jesus as a lifestyle. What a gift! You can let go and rest in His arms each moment and, at the same time, look forward to ultimate rest and intimacy with the Lord forever in eternity!

Strive to enter His rest. What a paradox, yet what a true adventure He offers. We strive to enter His rest by ceasing our own striving to make life work on our own. Essentially, striving to enter His rest is abiding.

Yet there is a serious warning in Hebrews, as in Revelation. I have the assurance of safety in His arms, yet I can freely choose to walk away from Him. That's why "hiding sideways" is nothing to take lightly. In turning away from intimacy with Him, I not only stop the flood of His light and love into my life, but I risk the possibility of drifting out of His embrace of grace. He will pursue me, always seeking to woo me back. His warning to Ephesus is still there for us. It's as if He is saying, "Turn back to me, or you will lose your light and way back to me." There is such a paradox: If we come to Him, He will give us rest—rest from running our own life, and if we turn away from Him, He will call to us, receiving us back with open arms. But if we continue turning and drifting away from intimacy with Him, there can come a day when it's too late.

Today is the day to hear His voice saying, "Come to me, turn back to me." He wants us to not harden our heart with an unyielded, prideful will. He wants us to yield our soft, believing hearts to His loving embrace. He wants us to abide. When we do, we will bear much fruit. This is His simple truth. Regardless of what the world says to you, accept His invitation.

Turn directly to the Lord and lament—crying out to Him. He would rather you get it off your chest and beat your fists on

His chest than have you go off in silent suffering, or whining to others in ever increasing melancholy and self-pity.

Hide from hiding from God. Hide in the shelter of His wings. Reject your fear of rejection and risk it all, unleashing the full fury of your pain on Him. You might be afraid of making Him mad or be even more afraid He doesn't care… or…is not there.

There is one haunting, central fear lurking deep in *every* human being. Some would say it is the fear of death. But I can show you people who are truly not afraid of death. Some would say it is the fear of suffering and dying, and it is true that some who are not afraid of death are indeed afraid of dying and the pain and disability that may precede it. Yet, I have met those who are truly unafraid of pain. They know there are worse things than pain, dying, and death.

Loneliness may be the most frequent and commonly uncomfortable feeling in every human being. It exposes the deepest fear of humanity—the fear of ultimate aloneness and destruction.

I have never met a person not shaken by the prospect of ending up ultimately all alone—if they really stop and think about it. It's something we don't want to mention or discuss. God Himself says in Genesis 2:18, "It is not good that man should be alone" (NKJV). In John 14, the night before His death on the cross, Jesus told His disciples He must "go away." Yet He sought to calm their central fear by saying, "I will not leave you orphaned." He promised to return (from the dead) and be with them always through the Holy Spirit. Romans 8:15 tells us that the Holy Spirit is the Spirit of adoption.

The Lord knows that the worst thing that can happen to us is to be left all alone, separated from Him. This is not an imagined, irrational fear. It is the central, legitimate fear of all humans because it is the worst that can ultimately happen. The everlasting torment of hell is not a social party—but separation. Jesus came in perfect love, offering Himself as the only way to find ultimate rest from ultimate aloneness in a loving secure relationship with Him forever!

And yet, this ultimate fear fuels all human activity that's not of the Living God. It "makes the world go 'round." This fear of aloneness drives our economy in general and drives us personally into the arms of evil—person by person, moment by moment. We get into so much trouble trying to fill our emptiness, looking for love in all the wrong places. And when the Devil sees us come to Jesus and turn away from the world, he tries desperately to distract us by tempting us to fill our emptiness with church activities—to settle for religion as a cheap substitute for Jesus.

When the Antichrist comes, he will play on believers' fears through right-sounding lies and promises of worldly security. Only those resting in Jesus' love will not be deceived. Fear is the "hook" of deception.

Fortunately Jesus, who came to rescue us and desires to be our First Love, attacks our core fear, pulling no punches. He exposes all our hiding when He says, "Don't be afraid of those who want to kill your body; they cannot touch your soul. Fear only God, who can destroy both soul and body in hell" (Matt. 10:28). He is not speaking about humans or the Devil. He is speaking of the Father. At first glance, it's not pleasant. We would rather look away. Our God can destroy us completely in utter separation from Him, and He has every right to do so! But as it says in Proverbs, "The fear of the Lord is the beginning of knowledge" (Prov. 1:7, NKJV). Jesus is out to do much more than just replace our many subordinate fears with acknowledgement of God's ability to destroy us.

Fortunately for us, Jesus says, "God sent his Son into the world not to judge the world, but to save the world through him" (John 3:17, NKJV). For all eternity, the hands that could destroy us are scarred from the nails He endured to save us. Jesus is not out to destroy you. He IS out to destroy your fear, the works of the devil, and the Devil himself. So, He is opening His arms to you right now. I can hear Him saying, "Turn back to Me, let's look together at your ultimate fear. My Father and I are One. I alone have been given the authority to condemn you to ultimate aloneness and destruction. Yet, I have chosen to take all that upon Myself for you. Accept the truth that I could destroy you. Accept the truth that I have instead chosen to save you. Most importantly, accept *Me*, and you will never be alone, never be destroyed. I will be with you always. I will never forsake you."

I beg you to stay in this sacred moment. First things first. No matter what is happening in your life right now, His loving eyes are looking deeply into your heart. Hear Him say, "Turn back to Me." Make the quarter turn into His full embrace. Fear not. Embrace and be embraced.

Let's Pray:

Lord, You know how I have been hiding from You. No one else may see how I willfully ignore You and Your ways. But You see... You see all my failures... and still You love me. Thank You from the bottom of my heart. Thank You from the bottom of the hole I dig for myself! Thank You for not giving up on me. Your love is relentless. I surrender! I now draw near to You. Please draw near to me. Please take me deeper into Your heart. This is new territory for me, but I want to stop hiding. Take me on great adventures of loving and living in You. Lead me to others who are hiding. Let's love them out of their caves as well! In Jesus' name, amen.

CHAPTER 12

FIRST
THINGS FIRST

Nevertheless I have this against you, that you have left your first love. Remember therefore from where you have fallen; repent and do the first works...

— *Revelation 2:4–5, NKJV*

What are the first works that flow from resting in Jesus as our First Love? There is one work that must come *first*, from which every other work must flow.

"Then they said to Him, 'What shall we do, that we may work the works of God?' Jesus answered and said to them, 'This is the work of God, that you *believe* in Him whom He sent'" (John 6:28–29, NKJV).

Did you notice here that Jesus says "the" work of God? In one sense, the only work we are called to do is believe in Jesus. Everything good from the Father is released from the well of our believing in Jesus.

In John 7:37–38 Jesus says, "If anyone thirsts, let him come to Me and drink. He who believes in Me, as the Scripture has said, out of his heart will flow rivers of living water" (NKJV).

Letting Jesus Love You

The rest of the first works are best understood as living water, the works of the Holy Spirit—in us and through us. After believing, the *first works* are the fruit and gifts of the Spirit growing and flowing into the world.

The fruit of the Spirit is the character of Christ growing in us, as described in Galatians 5:16–23. "So I say, let the Holy Spirit guide your lives... But the Holy Spirit produces this kind of fruit in our lives: love, joy, peace, patience, kindness, goodness, faithfulness, gentleness, and self-control."

Do you want the Spirit to grow the character of Christ in you? Come rest and let the Holy Spirit guide you.

The gifts of the Spirit are the power of Christ flowing through us as described in 1 Corinthians 12:4–11:

> There are diversities of gifts, but the same Spirit... But the manifestation of the Spirit is given to each one for the profit of all: for to one is given the word of wisdom... to another the word of knowledge... to another faith... to another gifts of healings... to another the working of miracles, to another prophecy, to another discerning of spirits, to another different kinds of tongues, to another the interpretation of tongues... distributing to each one individually as He wills (NKJV).

Do you want the Spirit to release the power of Christ in you? Come rest in Jesus' love and seek the gifts for Christ's sake.

First Corinthians 14:1 reads, "Let love be your highest goal! But you should also desire the special abilities the Spirit gives..."

The gifts of the Spirit are available to every believer. We are told to earnestly seek the gifts. In Luke 11, Jesus tells us to keep asking for more and more of the Holy Spirit. You ask and He will release the gifts sooner or later in you, as He sees fit. Keep on asking, keep on knocking, keep on seeking for more of the gifts—not for greed but for love!

The Lord loves to give us gifts, He just wants us to use them to help people, not hurt them. The gifts must be harnessed by His love. The Lord does not raise spoiled children. The Spirit will sometimes splash His manifest presence wherever He wills but He does not constantly release His power in people who are not humble and loving. The Lord does not lack power. He does lack the evidence of His character manifest in His people.

A wise old friend, Fran Wilcox, once suggested to me that the Heavenly Father delights in giving His gifts just like any parent on Christmas Day does. He delights in seeing us using our gifts. He knows that His children have to learn how to play with their gifts in a way that is safe for everyone. Once in a while His children are going to misuse the gifts and bop each other over the head, so to speak! He's not worried about that! His Spirit is there to discipline us in love.

Many are seeking a balanced life. One time the Lord put a picture in my mind to show me His idea of "balance" in a Christian's life. I saw balance scales with a "9" for nine gifts of the Spirit on one side and a "9" for nine fruit of the Spirit on the other side. Except, the nine fruit weighed heavier. I saw that the Lord cares more about seeing His character in us than releasing His power through us.

Let's be clear. The power gifts of the Holy Spirit do help us become more Christlike and, in fact, can increase the awe of the Lord in us and others. Some people greatly underestimate the value of the gifts and deny themselves the holiness of God's power. Christ had both divine character and power. To become like Him we, too, need both.

However, it's disastrous to overemphasize the gifts at the expense of character. As Paul says in 1 Corinthians 13:1–2,

Letting Jesus Love You

"Though I speak with the tongues of men and of angels, but have not love, I have become sounding brass or a clanging cymbal... [if I] have not love, I am nothing" (NKJV).

When I saw the vision of the scales, I heard the Lord say something in my heart: "You think My people are more afraid of the gifts of the Spirit than the fruit of the Spirit. That is not true. Yes, they are naturally afraid of what they have not yet experienced. Yes, they are afraid of how some have hurt others claiming to exercise the gifts. However, My people are actually more afraid of the fruit of the Spirit. They all say they want My fruit, but to bear My fruit, they must change. They have to die to themselves."

Wow! God is love. His power is love expressed. For First Love works to flow, we must keep first things first!

1. Rest secure in Jesus as your First Love.
2. Die to self and grow in Jesus' character.
3. Earnestly seek and flow in Jesus' power.
4. Love your neighbor as the Spirit leads.

CHAPTER 13

FREE TO FAIL

So if the Son makes you free, you will be free indeed.
— *John 8:36, NASB*

A few years ago, my son, Daniel, was a freshman in high school who loved football and *hated* math. What he hated more was having to come home on a spring afternoon to let us know that he had an *F* going in math with less than a month to go in the semester. My wife, Kim, was deeply concerned, but calm. I was just deeply concerned. So much for calm!

I issued a pronouncement that *F*s were not acceptable in our household and if he ended the semester with an *F*, there would be no football in the fall. As I left the room, I caught a glance of the tension on his face. I went downstairs, immediately realizing that this was not one of the highlights of my parenting history. I was rolling the matter around in my head when I felt led to pray. Guess who prompted that?

I simply cried out, "Lord, help me help Daniel." Immediately, the picture of a conversation with Bishop Rueben Job fourteen years earlier came into my mind. I had been just two months away from beginning as lead pastor of a church that some colleagues so "helpfully" described as a "preacher killer." The church had once held a position of great prestige, but had fallen onto hard times. On my introductory visit to the church, I sensed a "spiritual darkness" for which my theology did not make allowance. (Only later would I look back on the seven years I spent there and be able to recognize the spiritual warfare that was underway. I am so grateful for the Lord's protection in my ignorance. It is said that ignorance is bliss. Not true. His love toward our ignorance is bliss!)

Bishop Job was a prayerful man, one of the most Christlike men I have ever known. When he assigned me to the church, he said, "We are giving you a great challenge. We are not doing you any favors. No matter what happens, I want you to know one thing—you are free to fail." That meant so much to me at that moment, but only years later did I more fully grasp the grace and wisdom he shared. I'm sure he knew the truth he was speaking could only be fully understood after much trial and fire in life. He had gone through that fire and was now planting a timely seed.

Though I knew I had the bishop's backing, I still felt I had much to prove to myself and my competitive colleagues.

As my thoughts returned to my edict to Daniel, I heard Rueben's words one last time, "There is one thing I want you to know. You are free to fail."

As I heard his gentle words in my heart, I began to weep and repent of my harshness toward Daniel. I remembered Jesus' parable of the unforgiving debtor: A man is forgiven a large debt and then immediately refuses to release another person who owes him a much smaller debt. When the master who forgave the man's debt learns of this, he exclaims, "You evil servant! I forgave you that tremendous debt because you pleaded with me. Shouldn't you have mercy on your fellow servant, just as I had mercy on you?" (Matt. 18)

The grace once and forever extended to me I had withheld from my own dear son. I immediately turned away from all that harshness and went upstairs to find my son, who was still sitting, dejected, with my wife right where I left them.

I looked into my son's eyes and said, "Please forgive me, son. I was wrong. I love you. It does not matter if you get an F. I will never take football away from you. I am here to help you, but you are free to fail." In his eyes and on his face, I saw a mountainous burden lift off of him. He forgave me. We embraced, long and deep.

Then I told him, for the first time, of Rueben's words to me years earlier. I told him of Jesus' parable which, being a Bible lover, he already knew well. My son will never again (by God's grace) hear my condemnation for any of his failures.

By the way, once Daniel knew he was free to fail, he went out and finished the class with a passing grade. He went on to be first team all-state in football, winning a full college scholarship. He plays nose-tackle for Western Illinois University with a major in emergency management (not math!). Proud dad? Absolutely. But I'm ever more grateful for his tender heart for Jesus and people, as well as his ongoing love for the Bible. I'm most proud of his Heavenly Father, who stepped in when his earthly father was failing and needed a reminder!

One thing I have learned from the Lord through my failures is that I am not truly free until I am free to fail. And I am not free to fail until the One who holds authority over me says so. I am free to fail when Jesus frees me from my need to succeed. It's possible to be freed from the need to succeed the moment He says, "You are free to fail." But, for me, it took several years of failing in the strength of my own power, climaxed by my failure to respond gracefully to my son's F.

LETTING JESUS LOVE YOU

Where are you on the issues of success and failure, condemnation and mercy? Consider this. Isn't it something that the One who died on the cross for us was viewed as a failure by everyone around Him? Yet, in that moment He said, "It is finished!" The Greek word is *tetelestai* meaning "debt paid in full." What is it about *finished* we don't understand?

The next time your fear of failure shakes you into harshness toward others or yourself—the next time you catch yourself being a taskmaster trying to force yourself or another to prove something—remember this: everything that needed to be proven in your life was accomplished by Him on that cross.

Human striving for success is the wide road that leads to destruction. Even if none of your own dreams of grandeur ever come true in your life—the cross did! You are free to fail because He succeeded for you. Begin at the cross and rest there in the shadow of His wings. Let Him finish your life as He sees fit. You are not free to thrive until you know you are free to fail.

Isn't it interesting that the word *finished* begins with an *F*?

CHAPTER 14

SO MUCH MORE

Now all glory to God, who is able, through his mighty power at work within us, to accomplish infinitely more than we might ask or think.

— *Ephesians 3:20*

One winter day the snow fell generously and extravagantly from the sky. That's not usually a big deal in Iowa, but it was already the middle of January, and it was our first snow! I headed out to shovel our driveway and walks. As the garage door opened to reveal a blazing scene of white, I saw our neighbor out shoveling his driveway, "assisted" by his three small children. He towered above them, taking large scoops while they bounded around him like the Keystone Cops. Suddenly came the cry of cries from his little girl's heart—a cry that melted my heart, reaching the little boy within—a plea that instantly and completely captured my neighbor—"Daddy, Daddy, let's make a snowman!"

As I began to shovel my drive, my neighbor abandoned what was left of his and waded into the middle of his yard surrounded by shrieking kids. I was relieved to see that the six inches of snow were pretty light and powdery. Good for me...but not for snowmen!

74

Letting Jesus Love You

I looked over to see the father and his children, all on their knees, carefully pushing snow together and making progress, nonetheless. A closer look revealed that he was using a spray bottle to constantly wet the snow, showing the kids how to fashion the snowman, almost as a sculptor with clay. Amazing!

I called out, "Hey Dad, great day to be with your kids making snowmen!"

He replied almost breathlessly, "Yeah, it sure is!"

I called to the kids, "You sure have a wonderful dad to make a snowman with!" Their heads bobbed in assent. I said, "And I'm sure that your dad has wonderful kids!"

He said to them, "Say thank you," and they all complied... quickly so they could return to work on their snowman.

I went on with my shoveling. As I finished, I saw the father still at work—the kids long gone to new escapades. Their dad was finishing patting Mr. Snowman's midsection in place. I went inside, warmed up, and looked out a half hour later to see the dad alone, sculpting Mr. Snowman's head in his hands. A generous father caught up in finishing the job, caught up in being a child again himself.

That's how it works, isn't it? It's an amazing chain reaction of love. If a man listens only with his adult mind to a child's request for a snowman on a non-snowman day, He responds with an icy explanation as he denies the request—"It's not the right kind of snow." But when a father listens to his child's request with a heart of love, He wades in with all he has and does even more than the child can think or ask. Even if the child's attention span or frostbit cheeks fall short, the father stays at it and delivers so much more.

Jesus said, "You fathers—if your children ask for a fish, do you give them a snake instead? Or if they ask for an egg, do you give them a scorpion? Of course not! So if you sinful people know how to give good gifts to your children, how much more will your heavenly Father give the Holy Spirit to those who ask him?" (Luke 11:11–13)

There is one God who wants to pour Himself out completely for us. His loving heart is always ready to give so much more than we can think or ask. So stop, think, and ask—BIG—for God's richest blessing—Himself. Ask for the Holy Spirit to fill you to overflowing, and watch what happens. Your Father will pour out so much more of Himself than you dared think or ask.

Just ask, ask, ask, and keep asking—from the heart of the child deep inside of you.

CHAPTER 15

UNTOUCHABLE

And I give them eternal life, and they shall never perish; neither shall anyone snatch them out of My hand.

— *John 10:28, NKJV*

Don't be afraid of those who want to kill your body; they cannot touch your soul. Fear only God, who can destroy both soul and body in hell.

— *Matthew, 10:28*

I was lying on my face in worship. In my spirit, I saw myself being taken up higher and higher into the clear blue sky. Suddenly, something like a trap door opened in the sky and I went through it.

I found myself in a beautiful, sun-splashed meadow. I saw Jesus and ran to Him with childlike glee.

He scooped me up in His arms as if I were a toddler, and He held me high above His head. His smiling eyes looked up into mine as He said, "You are untouchable!"

How wonderfully ironic!

His hands—nailed for all the lepers, all the hemorrhaging women, all the tax collectors, all the prostitutes, all the cripples, all the blind, all the deaf, all the eunuchs, all the soldiers, all the winebibbers, all the gluttons, all the fishermen, all the lost sheep of Israel, all the Gentiles, and all of us "untouchables"—are the scarred hands that keep each believer safe and untouchable from evil.

How wonderfully ironic! The only One who can ultimately destroy you is the only One who can make the ultimate sacrifice to save you—and He did!

The One who has the power to crush you in His hands chose to let His hands be nailed for you.

The hands that healed untouchables are the hands that can keep you untouchable.

Come *rest* in the wonderful irony, spoken with smiling eyes, "You are untouchable."

When we have come to Jesus and have let Him convince us that we are untouchable, we become free to accept the second part of His great invitation: "Take my yoke upon you and learn from Me" (Matt. 11:29, NKJV). We are ready to truly let Jesus lead us.

PART 2:

LETTING JESUS
LEAD YOU

CHAPTER 16

THE OLD OX

Take My yoke upon you and learn from Me, for I am gentle and lowly in heart.

— *Matthew 11:29, NKJV*

The ox yoke is unfamiliar in our urbanized culture. However, ox training has not changed for oxen—or for followers of Christ.

In Jesus' day, ox yokes were hand-fashioned by carpenters who made them custom fit for two-oxen teams. A young ox would be harnessed to an older ox that had mastered the steady pace for carrying loads the long haul.

When first yoked, the young ox wants to lead but chafes at the yoke because of the plodding of the old ox. The old ox will not be rushed! Sometimes, the young ox has had enough and wants to dig in his heels to stop things. It chafes again because the old ox is now on a roll and the young ox can't get a foothold. The old ox will also not be stopped!

Jesus is the old ox. He has been through life, suffering, death, and resurrection. He knows how to carry the load of human existence for the long haul. He knows the "pace of grace." We don't. That's why He says, "Learn from Me." That phrase is full of grace. The Lord doesn't expect us to be perfect followers just because He is a perfect leader.

But can we stand to be led? The core issue of the yoke is control. When Jesus says, "Come to Me" with your burden, He asks you to trust Him in the moment. When He says, "Take *My* yoke" He asks you to give Him control of your future. The yoke includes all the fullness of relationship Jesus offers. Teacher to student. Lord to disciple. Father to child. Lover to beloved. Big brother to sibling. It's one thing to let Jesus rescue you; it's another thing to let Him do *all* He can do. Many Christians simply will not.

As you begin to let Jesus love you and lead you, He will help you "unlearn" many unscriptural thoughts and behaviors— in addition to teaching you all the good stuff. One common unscriptural way of thinking is this: the Lord is a harsh schoolmaster, threatening me with a yardstick or detention. Notice Jesus spoke to reassure us by saying, "I am gentle and lowly of heart." You can trust Him *because* He is gentle and humble toward you. He is fierce toward the forces of hell, but He is gentle toward humanity.

I am always in awe as I think of Jesus washing His disciples' feet (see John 13, NKJV). He said, "What I am doing you do not understand now" (v. 7). Isn't it amazing that our Lord's posture is on His knees, looking up into our faces? Scripture says He is not the *accuser* of the brethren, but the *firstborn* of many brethren. He doesn't lord *over* you, He leads from *beneath you.*

Jesus told Peter, "If I do not wash you, you have no part with Me" (v. 8). If you're going to let Jesus love you, then choose to see Him at your feet—looking up into your eyes with knowing love. When I do that, Jesus gently leads me past any walls of shame or fear into freedom and hunger to receive more from Him. The same *will* happen for you. You *will* receive His expansive heart of love, which *will* change you. Then you *will* want to generously release His love and watch as He wonderfully turns our world upside-down.

Jesus loves you *from* a servant position. You learn *from* Him when you gratefully humble yourself. You can only learn from Him by letting Him serve you and then you, in turn, serve others. Yet, of course, we know the Lord is worthy to be worshipped from our knees—right? It's "both and"! Looking up to Him means looking down at Him.

In this "school of rest" we all have so much to learn! That's because Jesus has so much love! The Lord always goes lower than you... to love you, to teach you, to lead you. He is always looking up at your whole being, including your weakness, and He loves you.

Much revelation awaits those who see that the young man in the Song of Solomon represents Jesus and the young woman represents believers. The young woman's skin is dark from sunburn because she was forced outdoors by her brothers' anger, but the young man sees her darkness as part of her beauty. Though her darkness is a stigma to the world, it is savory to her lover. Jesus loves our weakness because it is part of us and because it helps us realize our need for Him.

As you let the "old ox" lead, He will help you unlearn the way you thought He looked upon your weakness. He is looking up at you and loves *all* of you. I used to say, "Jesus loves me in spite of my weakness." Now I know Jesus loves *all* of me, including my weakness—because it's part of me! And it's the part that actually causes me to see my need for Him. He wastes no time pointing a finger...He uses my weakness to draw me closer so He can cleanse, heal, and teach me...and you.

When you let the Lord's love help you in your weaknesses, He is also there to help you unlearn your old habits.

COME REST

If you fear for provision or the esteem of others, you may be tempted to fearfully generate more income or reputation. But Jesus looks up at you and says, "Let me wash away your fear of man. I am your provider. I am your righteousness. Let go of your strategies. Let me show you what I want you to do." Suddenly, the urgent scheming fades and you can ask for His help and declare His promises anew.

If you are anxious or fatigued, the temptation of lust may be waiting at your door. Instead of opening the door to fantasy or media, listen for Jesus to say, "Let me wash away your fear of being all alone in this world. I am your Comforter. Hold onto Me. I will teach you rest and how to behave confidently in Me."

If you are wounded and nursing a grudge, the temptation of self-pity will often press upon you. Instead of blaming the world, hear Jesus reassure you, "Let me wash away your anger. Let go of the grudge. Step out of the judgment seat. Come rest in the mercy seat with me. I am your forgiver, learn to be a forgiver, too!"

As the young ox, I have chafed at much learning and unlearning under Jesus' patient, gentle yoke. When confronted by temptation, I used to shout, "Jesus, I love you more than this!" But then I discovered that sometimes those words were the feeble cry of my own pride striving to carry the load. It didn't work.

Now, when faced with temptation, I'm learning to close my eyes, look "down" into His eyes, and cry out in my weakness, "Jesus, *You* love me more than this! Help me, Lord!" He always does.

Though you or I sometimes act like a young ox, the Lord does not call us dumb! He calls us beautiful. Some say trust is earned, but with "the old ox," trust is learned.

LETTING JESUS LEAD YOU

Alright, "young ox," how about it? Are you ready to let go of control and enroll in His gentle school of love? The "old ox" is waiting.

Chapter 17

Filled or Crushed?

For My yoke is easy and My burden is light.

— *Matthew 11:30, NKJV*

In the movie, *The Abyss,* actor Ed Harris plays the part of Bud, the leader of a commercial deep sea diving company. Bud is enlisted by the U.S. government to retrieve nuclear weapons that have fallen deep down into a crevice in a trench in the ocean floor. The crevice is so deep that Bud must don a diving suit that looks like that of an astronaut.

In the most compelling scene of the movie, Bud has to allow his diving suit to be completely filled with oxygenated liquid—he actually has to breathe in the liquid to fill his lungs. This is because the outside pressure of the ocean at that depth would crush his body if it had any air pockets. Harris is assured that once his lungs are filled, he will be fine and able to maneuver effectively down in the crevice. The problem is that as he begins to breathe in the liquid, his body will naturally resist with a drowning reflex and tremendous panic.

LETTING JESUS LEAD YOU

Throughout the process he is encouraged to trust that he will be okay, for the oxygen will kick in and sustain him. Though the process is excruciating, he keeps "letting go," and eventually he is at peace, lungs and suit filled. In the next scene, he exits the submarine and leaps off into the abyss, for the sake of others, not knowing how deep he may have to go.

Jesus said, "My way is easy." But it's easy to believe Jesus' way is anything but easy! He tells us to pick up our cross and follow Him. He also tells us we will have trouble. Therefore, *easy* does not mean lack of trouble or lack of sacrifice. *Easy* means "custom fit"—His way of life for us is relational and *personal.* When we have received Him, His Spirit is *inside* us—ready to relate to us and ready to release His power as we *relate* to Him.

Notice Jesus says *My* burden is light. Many people say the Lord has given them a burden for this or that. I understand them to mean the Lord has given them His heart for a particular cause. But often they seem to have a heaviness and lack of lightheartedness. That's not what Jesus wants. His burden is *light.* Following Christ is not meant to be burdensome and dreary. Many believers become weary because they take on a load that Jesus did not intend for them to carry alone. They go on carrying that cruel load with the thought that Jesus wants them to be so miserable! But what He truly desires is to *so empower* them that what would have been heavy for the natural man becomes light. He wants us to walk *with Him*, and when we move in concert, our burden is indeed light!

I love how Eugene Peterson has translated Matthew 11:30 in The Message. "Keep company with me and you'll learn to live freely and lightly." Yeah! That's what Jesus is talkin' about!

Yet how does that fit with carrying our cross? Isn't my cross heavy and unbearable? You bet—if I try carrying it on my own. But if Jesus lives in me and if I ask Him to fill me over and over again with the power of the Holy Spirit, then His life *inside me* is more than enough to withstand the pressures coming against me. The Bible says, "Greater is He who is in you than he who is in the world" (1 John 4:4, NASB). Yielding to the Lord is like breathing in oxygenated liquid. In fact, notice what Jesus did to impart the Holy Spirit in John 20. He breathed on the disciples!

When we "breathe Him in," when we deny self and prayerfully submit to what the Bible says—His way of life can cause our flesh to panic in a "drowning reflex." But as we let go in Him, the Holy Spirit will breathe in us to be our rest and our peace, strong enough to stand against any pressure that comes at us from the outside.

That's why Paul could say, "We are hard-pressed on every side, yet not crushed; we are perplexed, but not in despair; persecuted, but not forsaken; struck down, but not destroyed—always carrying about in the body the dying of the Lord Jesus, that the life of Jesus also may be manifested in our body" (2 Cor. 4:8–10, NKJV).

So come…

breathe…

die to self…

live freely and lightly.

LETTING JESUS LEAD YOU

LET'S PRAY:

Lord, I have a lot to learn. Some days I am a bundle of energy wanting to go several directions at once. Other days I just want to chuck it all. Once in a while I feel like I am following Your lead, but those days are fewer than I'd like. I'm tired of guesswork. I want to know You and Your ways. I give You my heart, cluttered and willful as it is. I repent of filling myself full of junk food, junk media, junk talk, and junk thinking. Cleanse and soften my heart so I can sense the slightest whisper of Your voice, the gentlest nudge of Your hand. I want to follow You. Teach me Your pace of grace. I want You. I want to eat, drink, and breathe Your love. This is a little scary, but here goes. I'm selling out to You completely. I trust You to take care of my business, I'm going to be all Yours. Lead on! Amen.

CHAPTER 18

WHO'S RESPONSE-ABLE?

Then Moses said to the LORD, "See, You say to me, 'Bring up this people.' But You have not let me know whom You will send with me. Yet You have said, 'I know you by name, and you have also found grace in My sight.' Now therefore, I pray, if I have found grace in Your sight, show me now Your way, that I may know You and that I may find grace in Your sight. And consider that this nation is Your people."

And He said, "My Presence will go with you, and I will give you rest."

Then he said to Him, "If Your Presence does not go with us, do not bring us up from here. For how then will it be known that Your people and I have found grace in Your sight, except You go with us? So we shall be separate, Your people and I, from all the people who are upon the face of the earth."

So the LORD said to Moses, "I will also do this thing that you have spoken; for you have found grace in My sight, and I know you by name."

— Exodus 33:12–17, NKJV

Letting Jesus Lead You

This is an amazing conversation between Moses and God! Moses had just led the people of Israel out of slavery in Egypt, with God's power paving the way. They were now camped at a crossroads at Mt. Sinai. God's presence had descended upon the mountain to teach them how to obey and worship Him in holiness so that His presence could come to dwell permanently with them. But Moses was nervous. The people were stubborn and weak. They were glad to be rescued from Pharaoh, but they didn't really want to come very close to this Deliverer God. Moses knew that the Lord wanted him to prepare the people to conquer the Promised Land, but he felt alone and inadequate as he confronted the Lord.

Moses basically said, "Lord, I need better helpers! I need to know your plans! I need *all* of You because I'm not up to this! Remember, these people are Your responsibility!" Moses enjoyed such intimacy with the Lord that he could be boldly honest in his anxiety about the future. There is a lot of grace in that for you and me. The Lord is not anxious about our anxiety. He does not feel inadequate to deal with our inadequacy.

Think about this. The Lord's answer to your every cry of aloneness and inadequacy is, "I will go with you—and I will give you rest from every threat!"

Wow!

Who needs miserable companions like Fear and Self-pity? Let's kick them off the bus! We need only one yokefellow—the Lord. If God is for us, who can be against us?

The Lord said to Moses, "My Presence will go with you, and I will give you rest" (Ex. 33:14). Certainly the Lord had this in mind in Matthew 11:28 when He said, "Come to me... and I will give you rest." The Hebrew word for "rest" used here in Exodus 33 is *nuach*. The same word is used sixty-five times in the Old Testament. It has double usage. Isaiah 11:2 says of the coming Savior, "The Spirit of the Lord shall *rest* upon

Him" (NKJV). The Lord gives us rest as the Holy Spirit comes to rest upon us! "Come Rest" is a two-way street. When we come rest in Jesus, the Holy Spirit comes to rest on us, and the Kingdom of God advances wherever we let Him lead us. *Rest* is not a passive state of solitude but a dynamic gift of trusting companionship *with* the Lord! *Rest* is freedom from fear so that we can boldly defeat the enemy and take the Promised Land.

Are you at a crossroad of aloneness and inadequacy? The Lord will actually lead you to this crossroad several times in life, where you must honestly and desperately seek and rely upon only Him. In one sense, it is a daily dilemma with only one answer. Do you hunger for the Lord and settle for nothing less than Him, or do you keep pining and whining and settling for something much less?

Do you put all your "faith eggs" in His basket, or do you spread them around? He is a jealous God. He wants us to place *all* our faith in Him. He never says in Scripture, "Have faith in each other." He says, "Love one another" (John 13:34, NKJV). The Lord wants to give us rest from placing heavy burdens of expectations upon ourselves and others. The Scriptures say that Jesus did not trust people because He knew what was in their hearts. The Lord does something better than trusting us; He loves us!

So copy Him. Love people instead of laying burdens on them. Try this. Stop relying on yourself or others' performance for your well-being. Love them anyway. Love yourself anyway. God does. Let God be God. When someone lets you down, it's an opportunity to forgive them and love them unconditionally! Even if you falter, His love for you will not.

Lower your anxious expectations of others and yourself to zero, and raise your hungry, desperate expectations of God to the max! Moses remembered that the people were ultimately God's responsibility, not his. Moses needed to respond to God's call, while God's job was to decide and secure the Israelites' destiny.

We do such burdensome things with the word *responsible*, as if it means "able to sustain and save." The word literally means only "able to respond." We have the God-given ability to respond to His saving love. However, we are not able to save and sustain our own lives and destinies. We are not "response-able" for our salvation or the salvation of others.

We are called to be *responsive* to the One who took *respons-ability* for us. Jesus, our Redeemer, took responsibility *for* us by paying the penalty for our sins on the cross and purchasing our freedom from slavery to the Devil with the ransom of His blood and sacrificial death. When we respond to this good news by letting Jesus come into our hearts as Lord and Savior, He responds by making us new people, and we are adopted into His family forever. Our old "me" has died and the new "me" is now an "us" (Christ living in us, Christ living for us, and us living for Christ).

Galatians 2:19–20 says, "My old self has been crucified with Christ. It is no longer I who live, but Christ lives in me. So I live in this earthly body by trusting in the Son of God, who loved me and gave himself for me." My daughter Emily says it this way, "Jesus, be my everything!" She means it. I watch the way she lives and I am reminded of what Jeremiah said in Lamentations 3:24, "The LORD is my portion" (NKJV).

Moses wanted God to be his everything, yet he had fear that somehow God might fail him. Isn't that the honest truth for all of us at some time or another?

God understands. He knows we need reassurance again and again. Look again at His conversation with Moses. In Exodus 33:14 the Lord assured Moses of His personal companionship and security—yet Moses continued his harangue anyway!

COME REST

Have you ever been all psyched up to argue a point with someone and, after you made your first pitch, heard them say, "OK, you win! Let's do it your way"? It usually takes all the wind out of your sails! But not for Moses. He was so anxious and keyed up to make his point that even when God told him He would go with him—Moses just barreled on. "Yeah, well, I hear You, but I'm telling You I'm not going unless You truly do what You say You're going to do!" Notice that God didn't get offended by such honest intimacy. He doesn't like us complaining to others about Him, but when we are serious about having it out with Him, He is serious about hearing us out...and revealing Himself. Jeremiah 29:13 says, "And you will seek Me and find Me, when you search for Me with all your heart" (NKJV).

Moses put it *all* out there, and God was so moved that He granted Moses' request to see Him. God lovingly passed by and let Moses see Him in *all* His goodness. If God were to show Moses everything, including His wrath, Moses would have been destroyed. This is the same Lord who eventually took responsibility by taking *all* His wrath and death upon Himself at the cross so that we might have *all* His mercy and eternal life.

You and I will always be inadequate to guide and sustain ourselves—that's actually good news! Accept it. At every crossroad you can cry out to the Cross Bearer who died for you and lives to be your Rest Giver. Rest from being your own savior. You've already got one.

CHAPTER 19

ROOM ENOUGH

Abandoning that one, he dug another well, and the local people finally left him alone. So Isaac called it "Room Enough" for he said, "At last the Lord has made room for us, and we will be able to thrive."

— *Genesis 26:22*

Isaac moved into the valley of Gerar after redigging the old wells of his father Abraham. This time he also dug three new wells.

At the first well, the water was good, but the locals argued with Isaac. So he named the well *Ezek*, meaning "argument," and moved on.

At the second well, the water was good, but the locals opposed him. So he named the well *Sitnah*, meaning "opposition," and moved on.

But at the third well, the locals neither argued nor opposed him. So he named the well *Rehoboth*, meaning "room enough." He said, "Here we will have room enough to be able to thrive."

This symbolizes what the Holy Spirit is searching for in us. All the Lord asks of us is that we neither argue with each other nor oppose His Word. That gives room enough for His presence to come and thrive in our midst! If we repent of rebellion, the Lord will grace us for obedience. If we repent of division, He will grace us for unity!

The Lord desires His bride, His people, to be without spot and blemish—rebellion and division.

Do you want to make room for Him in your life, your family, your church, your business, your nation? Learn from Him. Remember, He is *gentle* and *lowly of heart*. Those are the two virtues He wants to grow in you to replace argument and rebellion. Make room enough for Him. Let the Holy Spirit come and thrive.

The Lord desires His people to make room for Him so they can be His resting place. Isaiah 66:1–2 says,

Thus says the LORD, "Heaven is My throne and the earth is My footstool. Where then is a house you could build for Me? And where is a place that I may rest? For My hand made all these things, Thus all these things came into being," declares the LORD. "But to this one I will look, To him who is humble and contrite of spirit, and who trembles at My word" (NASB).

LET'S PRAY:

Jesus ebb and Jesus flow
May Your love rise within my soul.
Jesus ebb and Jesus flow
Let Your love rise within my soul.
Amen.

CHAPTER 20

SUB-MISSION

God resists the proud, but gives grace to the humble. Therefore submit to God. Resist the devil and he will flee from you.

— *James 4:6-7, NKJV*

Many times I have heard people say, "Resist the Devil and he will flee." But I have heard people address the Devil in warfare prayer with no effect. I have ministered to people who were devastated from resisting evil in their own willpower. And many times I have personally tried to resist evil with my will and failed. The Bible doesn't just say resist the Devil. The Bible says first, *submit to God.*

It is true that as children of the Father, by adoption through faith in Christ, we can say to all the forces of evil, "My dad can beat up your dad." However, don't go fighting other dads alone! The Bible says our God actually *resists* us in our pride. We cannot rid ourselves of rebellion and division. He gives the grace to fight evil only to the humble—those who submit to Him.

John 7:38 says, "He who believes in me, as the Scripture has said, out of his heart will flow rivers of living water" (NKJV).

COME REST

Submission is the faucet that releases living water. There is something in us that does not like the word *submission.* That something doesn't like to be told what to do. That something craves speaking and acting at the expense of others in a vain attempt to make ourselves feel more secure. That something is our sin nature.

Think about the word, "sub-mission." In a play on words, if I submit to you, then I am putting myself under your "mission." If I bow or kneel before you, I give you leverage over me. I am exposed and vulnerable. If I give you control, I will naturally be fearful… unless I also give you my trust. I know you will never harm me—*if* you love me perfectly and if you perfectly exercise the control I have given you.

However, there is only one Person who loves us perfectly and can be trusted to perfectly exercise the control we give. He is the Lord. He is Love. His *mission* is to be perfect love at all times.

In one sense, He is the only One to whom we are to submit in complete trust. Any time we submit to others is simply a momentary expression of our deeper submission to Jesus. Turn away from your sin nature and put yourself under His nature, His mission, His perfect love. Give Him leverage and control. He is the only One who can perfectly handle your life.

Even so, five times in the New Testament God's Word tells us to submit to other humans, both believers and unbelievers. I might be able to trust Him to take perfect care of me, but why does He expect me to submit to another human who has the same nasty sin nature I have?

Because. When I put your welfare, authority, or mission ahead of mine I am honoring Jesus for dying for me. Every time the Father sees His children imitate the Son, the Father delightfully dispatches the Holy Spirit to move in us, through us, over us, and around us… helping us to overcome our "natural" fear. He supernaturally fills us with the love and power of Jesus… and the kingdom advances "on earth as it is in heaven."

When I lovingly submit to you, trusting Him, even if you blow it and hurt me, He will turn it around for our good. I want to keep submitting to a Dad like that; how about you?

Pride resists submission, pride doesn't resist the Devil. Submission is the faucet that releases living water. Humble yourself, submit to God, resist the Devil and he will flee under the assault of the Holy Spirit.

When we submit to God and imitate His ways, resistance is *not* futile.

CHAPTER 21

ON EAGLE'S WINGS

Like an eagle that rouses her chicks
and hovers over her young,
so he spread his wings to take them up
and carried them safely on his pinions.

— Deuteronomy 32:11

One day in the middle of a long cold winter, the sun came out and warmed our city. The bright blue sky and streams of melting snow provided a glimpse of approaching spring. As we were leaving a noon prayer gathering for the salvation of lost people in our city, a young pastor friend, Caleb, asked if we could meet sometime to talk about ways he could improve his prayer life. What a mighty man of God in the making! It is always a privilege to be with someone hungry for Jesus.

Are you longing for more of Jesus? Ask Him for more. If you're not hungry, ask Him to fire hunger within you. Keep asking! Watch what happens.

As Caleb and I walked out to the parking lot, we scheduled a time to meet. Before we went to our cars I offered him Mother Theresa's famous counsel, "Begin where you are." I asked him to prepare for our meeting by reflecting on his prayer relationship and spiritual disciplines with the Lord. What was working and what was not working?

I wanted him to listen to himself…and the Lord! Sometimes things don't work in prayer because we are distracted by issues for which we need the Lord's help. But at other times, holy habits that once worked simply work no longer—our heart is no longer in them. That's because the Lord has taken our heart away from those practices. In the past, they may have been good habits that helped us go deeper with the Lord. But when God sees us depending on habits more than we depend on *Him*—He will pull them away just like eagles tending the nest of their young.

It is true that eagles carry their young on their backs to train them how to fly and to remove them from peril. But it is also true that when it's time to leave the nest, the parents pull out the bottom of the nest one twig at a time! That's how the Lord often leads us along. He pulls the bottom out, yet is always ready to bear us up!

Caleb was intrigued. I invited him to let the Lord meet him where he was and begin from there. Just before we parted, I looked up to the sky and saw two bald eagles soaring in an upward spiral above the city, the wind beneath their wings. What a confirming moment of awe for both of us!

Sometimes you may feel spiritually dry. You may have a sense of the Lord's absence rather than His presence. He is wooing you to go deeper, to hunger and thirst even more for Him. This is what it means to wait on Him.

But those who wait on the LORD Shall renew their strength;
They shall mount up with wings like eagles,
They shall run and not be weary, They shall walk and not faint
(Isa. 40:31, NKJV).

COME REST

You were made to surrender to the Lord, to rest in His love the way an eagle is made to stretch out its wings and rest on the wind. Eagles do little flapping and striving to rise. When eagles rest on the wind they are picked up by the wind to soar in ever upward spirals. A spiral is not a flat circle, but ever turning *forward*. Don't be surprised if, over the years, the Spirit leads you back to holy habits and disciplines He once led you away from. It's not that He is leading you back; He's leading you forward to an old discipline so the new you in new circumstances will benefit you in a new way!

When He says, "Follow me," He means it. He is God on the move! *Resting in His love* means to let Him lead us as He seeks the lost.

In Luke 5:10 Jesus says, "Don't be afraid! From now on you'll be fishing for people!" Just as eagles' wings are made for resting and rising, so eagles' eyes are made for seeing more deeply and precisely the higher they rise. Evangelism doesn't have to be as fearsome and heavy as we make it.

As you wait on the Lord and follow His lead, Jesus will teach you to fish for men—not like men, but like eagles! Eagles rise for one main reason, to hunt. An eagle lets the wind carry it just high enough to see a fish in the river. Then it closes its wings and lets gravity pull it down to its prey.

If you pray big for lost people around you to be saved and pray big for divine appointments with people who do not know Christ, the Spirit will fill you and lead you with love to those people He wants you to witness to and love. The main difference between Jesus' followers and eagles is we are to rest and rise in the Spirit to love and pray for the lost—not attack the lost as our prey.

Amazing things happen when we yield to the Lord. From the Lord's perspective, it's easy for Him to grow us spiritually. From our perspective spiritual growth is hard, because our stubborn wills make it hard. When you first receive Christ, the Holy Spirit comes in and immediately begins to change you. If you choose to resist Him, you actually have to work hard to not grow! The Spirit is in us, prompting us to respond with faith, hope, and love in every circumstance. He leads us into each day. He is prompting us to rest our "wings on the wind." As we choose to respond to each person or circumstance with faith, hope, and love, He changes us to be more like Christ! However, we often choose to flap and strain in our own power, often going "against the wind." We allow our responses to be filled with doubt, despair, and self-interest.

I'm not saying that spiritual growth is not a struggle. Of course He calls us to constantly step out of our comfort zone. He says, "Follow me!" not "Stand still!" But Jesus means what He says, "My yoke is easy and my burden is light." When we look at a tough situation, we sometimes anticipate with dread what will happen next. However, when we do it Jesus' way, it's amazing how He swiftly ushers us through.

Yes, it's often hard to choose to forgive, to choose to trust, to choose to be patient, to choose to be thankful, to choose to be faithful, to choose to be loving. However, when we make these hard choices regardless of circumstances, the Holy Spirit lifts us and propels us onward and upward. It's actually far easier than choosing to not do it Jesus' way.

It was such a "cool" moment with my friend that winter day! You should have been there! On second thought...you should begin where *you* are. The Lord does. Wait on the Lord and stretch out your wings. The winds of the Spirit won't leave you there long.

You have seen...how I bore you on eagles' wings and brought you to Myself.

— Exodus 19:4, NKJV

CHAPTER 22

LOVE KILLS

Our old sinful selves were crucified with Christ so that sin might lose its power in our lives.

— *Romans 6:6*

Only one thing kills sin and births a pure heart—God's loving presence.

In 1999, an itinerate prayer ministry team came to our church to teach on spiritual warfare. At the end of the seminar, our teacher, Vicky Porterfield, invited us to stand and ask the Holy Spirit to give us all He wanted to give us. What a "dangerous" thing to ask! I did. Suddenly, a swirling, sweet energy came upon me and dropped me into the pew! I immediately felt my tongue moving against the roof of my mouth. I focused on that a moment, shut it down, yet thought, "Oh God, it's all true." Suddenly, scenes from the Holy Spirit moving in the book of Acts and entries from John Wesley's journal began flooding my mind. This was the outpouring of the Spirit upon a hungry heart.

I remained in speechless awe for an hour. Then I was helped to the floor and experienced waves of laughter for almost another hour. In one beautiful touch, God had shown me more of Himself. Because of the blood of Jesus, I already knew He loves me just as I am. But it was awesome to experience Him more as *He is*. There is always more of Him to know and love! He is nobody to mess with, but He is also gentle and loves to play and laugh.

Many people call experiences like mine "being slain in the Spirit." Such happenings make some people nervous. I understand. Many are afraid of "being carried away." That's OK. You shouldn't let anyone carry you away—except God! Are you willing for that?

When God's presence comes, it's messy—we often fumble in grace. But it's much better to have a church full of His presence stumbling after Jesus—rather than a church full of people stuck proudly in sterile doctrines, empty of His infectious presence. The Holy Spirit comes where He is invited by imperfect people who want to love Him *as He is*. His love is His power. His power is His love.

In Revelation 2:1–7, Jesus rebukes the church of Ephesus and calls them back to Him as their First Love. Though they were effective at resisting heresy and immorality, they were also resistant to true intimacy with Jesus, and they were devoid of His powerful works. Truth *minus* His intimacy equals fearful doctrine; truth *plus* His intimacy equals love manifest.

In touching me, the Lord taught me about Himself. He touches people because they ask *and* because He wants to kill something and birth something else in them.

The next day, Vicky preached to the congregation. She held up a bottle of water and said, "If I told you that this contains 98 percent purified water and only 2 percent raw sewage, would you drink it?" Yuck. Then she said, "When you receive Jesus, the Holy Spirit comes to live in you. But He is holy. He does not want to inhabit a temple filled with sin. He hates your sin because He loves you. Your sin is hurting you and others. He has so much for you, if only you will let Him get rid of your sewage. What is *your* 2 percent?"

At that moment I was *truly* slain. Being slain in the Spirit is not about falling down; it's about falling deeper in love with Jesus. During the following year, God showed me my two percent and how to let His love kill it.

The Holy Spirit often begins with the pastor when He cleanses a church. If the pastor won't let Jesus cleanse his or her two percent, it's not likely to happen in the congregation. Conversely, when lay people let the Lord kill their sin, He gives them the supportive, prayerful heart for which every pastor aches to have around.

What is your two percent? Let Him help you face it. Let Him kill it with His love.

LET'S PRAY:

Lord, my 2 percent seems to be concentrated in the following areas: _____. Please forgive me and cleanse me completely. Holy Spirit, please give me all You want to give me right now. Make me more like Jesus.

(Rest in silence with Him for a moment.)

Amen.

CHAPTER 23

FREE AND CLEAR

Have faith in God. I assure you that you can say to this mountain, "May God lift you up and throw you into the sea," and your command will be obeyed. All that's required is that you really believe and do not doubt in your heart. Listen to me! You can pray for anything, and if you believe, you will have it. But when you are praying, first forgive anyone you are holding a grudge against, so that your Father in heaven will forgive your sins, too.

— *Mark 11:22-25*

The Lord shows us three things that can clog our souls and prevent the flow of the Holy Spirit into others' lives—three things that keep us from being true friends of sinners— three things that smother the loving faith God uses to move mountains:

- Nourished doubt
- Cherished unforgiveness
- Other unrepented sin

Come Rest

Letting Go of Nourished Doubt

"Don't be faithless any longer. Believe!" (John 20:27)

We nourish doubt by agreeing with worldly ideas that are not in the Bible. Many of us say, "It's healthy to doubt." No, it's not! There is not one place in the Bible that puts doubt in a positive light. I once heard revival preacher Sergio Scataglini say, "If you are going to doubt something—doubt your doubts. Trust the Lord."[1]

Late one night, in the spring of 1999, I was reading the autobiography of Billy Graham. I learned that early in his ministry he went out to the edge of a forest, opened his Bible, and laid it on a tree stump. He knelt and repented before God for arguing with, doubting, and theologizing God's Word. From that moment on, he professed his belief in every word of the Bible and dedicated his life to living according to and faithfully preaching God's Word.[2] The Holy Spirit pierced my heart. It was like Jesus coming to Thomas saying, "Don't be faithless any longer. Believe!" I was so tired of independent cynicism, which at its root is simply a fear of rejection. I could sense Him offering me the peace of His easy yoke.

I got on my knees and repented for all my "creative" theologizing and doubting of God's Word. I asked the Lord to help me, from that moment on, to submit every detail of my life to every word of His book.

At that point, I was forty-two years old, had been a pastor for twenty years, and had never read the Bible cover to cover.

---

1   Sergio Scataglini, sermon preached at the Breakthrough in the Heartland Conference, First Assembly of God, Cedar Rapids, Iowa, November 8, 1999.
2   Billy Graham, *Just As I Am: The Autobiography of Billy Graham*, (New York: HarperCollins, 1997).

LETTING JESUS LEAD YOU

I had attempted a few times and been easily put off track by distractions and sloth.

But this time was different. Conviction and repentance ignited a fiery hunger in me to read and feed on His Word. I desired, as John Wesley encouraged, to search each word with my heart. I began to see the Lord looking over my shoulder every time I opened the Bible. I learned to ask, "Jesus, please speak to me through Your Word." Then I would simply begin where I had last left my Bible's ribbon marker. I called it "pushing the ribbon."

I would read until a word or phrase touched my heart. Then I would stop and let the Lord converse with me. (You can know it's the Lord talking to you when the thoughts that come are loving, clear, and scriptural.) The simplicity was so freeing. In repenting from doubt, the Lord helped me make room enough inside for Him. He then filled me with hunger and expectation for Him to speak to me through every single word. Suddenly, I wasn't getting bogged down in Leviticus and Numbers! Every word was alive with the love of Jesus Christ. New insight, more peace, and thrilling questions seeking more insight began to flow. His Word really is alive!

Try it right now. Repent of your doubt of any word of Scripture and ask the Lord to fire a new hunger in your heart for feeding on His Word. Then, open the Bible, asking Jesus to speak to your heart through the next words you read. Read until something touches you. Stop and rest there. Trust that the insight and faith-seeking questions that come to your mind are the voice of the Lord spurring you on—calling you deeper into His love.

Release your doubt to Him, and He will release His gift of faith in you—faith to move mountains!

COME REST

LETTING GO OF CHERISHED UNFORGIVENESS

It's huge that Jesus calls us to repent of the sin of unforgiveness before He deals with us on every other sin.

In my own life and ministry, I have experienced the corrosion of unforgiveness in body and soul. Time and again, when I join with someone in prayer for their physical healing, the Lord reveals a deeper need for emotional healing. The Lord has shown me that there is a direct connection between unforgiveness and many forms of incurable and chronic disease. I saw the Lord take one person back sixty years in order to heal a memory, enabling him to forgive someone. After this, the "terminal" cancer was easy to pray off the person. The Lord turned that person's heaviness to joy. The Lord will never fail to turn the heaviness of your wounded unforgiveness into unbridled joy—if you let Him.

Let's say there is a sewer rat in the corner, and I hate that sewer rat so much that I swallow rat poison! Who gets hurt? I do. Unforgiveness kills! Jesus commands us to forgive because He loves us. He is not trying to place a burden on us. He is trying to take one off.

Colossians 3:13 says, "Remember, the Lord forgave you, so you must forgive others." What a wonderful verse of mercy and understanding from the Lord. He knows we all want to hurt those who hurt us. He knows we may resist taking action toward them, but we often cherish inward hostility toward them. He knows it may be buried, but it is not dead. He knows that only He can cleanse unforgiveness out of our souls and bodies.

He says, "Remember, I forgave you." Forgiveness is a grateful act of one's liberated will. Total forgiveness can only come from a heart that belongs to Jesus. Only Jesus living in me can help me truly forgive with no strings attached.

112

LETTING JESUS LEAD YOU

Because Jesus is not holding my sins against me, I can choose to no longer hold others' sins against them. I can let my grudge go to Jesus, ask Him to heal the wound, and ask Him to bless them. He loves when I do that, and He blesses me in return. In forgiving, I also close a window to spiritual attack from the Evil One.

I call this process of prayer the "Forgiver's Flowchart." It goes like this:

Give Him thanks →

Give Him your pain →

Give Him the grudge →

Give them mercy →

Receive His mercy and healing →

Pray blessing on them →

Give Him thanks again!

If you are having trouble forgiving someone, remember what forgiveness is and what it is not. Forgiveness is *not* something you do after you stop hurting. Forgiveness is something you do while you are still hurting. In fact, the wound cannot heal and the anger will not go until you forgive.

Think of the word "for-give" as a play on words. You *give* mercy *before* you feel like it. You *give* away your right to hurt someone back *before* they deserve it. You *give* them the love of Jesus because He died to forgive you all your sins *before* anyone ever hurt you.

Making yourself forgive does not mean you make yourself forget. Jesus will heal your memory and turn it into a reason for praise. He is the miracle man!

Do you want to try it? First of all, let Jesus in to be your Lord. Then let Him help you do the most Christlike thing you can ever do—forgive!

COME REST

Let go, rest in His love, and pray like this…

Jesus, thank You for dying for my sins. You are my Lord.
In Your blood, I have complete forgiveness forever.
You know the wound that _____ has caused me.
You know my pain and anger.
You know what I am holding in my heart against _____.
In the safety of Your presence, I give You my pain and anger.
I step out of the judgment seat, and I declare that You are in the
*   mercy seat!*
I let go of my grudge and I forgive_____.
Please touch my wound and heal me and take my anger away.
I ask You to bless _____ and give him/her abundant life in
*   Your name.*
Thank You, Lord! Amen.

UNREPENTANT SIN

This category is named *unrepentant*, which means "sinful habits" that are alive and well in our lives. They are continuing behaviors that we have not sought forgiveness for *and* we keep repeating. Saying we are sorry is only the beginning of repentance. Repentance is complete when the behavior is forgiven by God and ended by us! It's so good to let the Lord help us look at what still needs forgiveness and complete victory. Remember, He's not pointing a finger, so let Him love you through this inventory and repentance process.

Everything that is not good for us—every sin—falls into one of three categories. First John 2:16 says, "For all that is in the world—the lust of the flesh, the lust of the eyes, and the pride of life—is not of the Father but is of the world" (NKJV).

Lust of the flesh is hedonism—trying to comfort ourselves through our senses. We want pleasure to kill our *pain*.

Lust of the eyes is coveting—trying to comfort ourselves through possessions. We want financial "security" to kill our *fear*.

Pride of life is independence—trying to comfort ourselves through striving. We want control to kill our *despair*.

Our sin nature is triggered by pain, fear, and despair. We turn our eyes away from Jesus, the Light, and open our eyes to darkness...yet His eyes of love never waver. So turn your eyes back to Him and let Him have your pain, fear, and despair.

Some say, "You are what you eat." But Jesus says, "You become what you look at."

> The lamp of the body is the eye. If therefore your eye is good, your whole body will be full of light. But if your eye is bad, your whole body will be full of darkness. If therefore the light that is in you is darkness, how great is that darkness! (Matt. 6:22–23)

When you look at an object, you are physically letting light reflect the image of the object onto your brain. You are letting the image "in." Your soul is inextricably related to your body in this life. Your soul is the sum of your intellect, emotions, and will. What's good for your soul is good for your body and vice versa. If the image is something the Lord knows is good for you, then your body and soul will become healthier.

What's good for you? Simply put, whatever the Bible says is good for you. A good filter Scripture is Philippians 4:8: "And now, dear brothers and sisters, one final thing. Fix your thoughts on what is true, and honorable, and right, and pure, and lovely, and admirable. Think about things that are excellent and worthy of praise."

When the Bible says, "If therefore your eye is good..." the word *good* also means "clear." If you let Jesus help you keep your eyes clean and clear, then you will be filled with His light, His powerful presence. But, if you don't let Jesus wash you with His love and don't let Him lead you in making good choices about what to look at—your eyes will become cluttered with filth and darkness so that none of His power gets into you—then your body and soul will become dank, dark, and unhealthy.

Window blinds protect one's privacy, but if they are never opened one's house cannot be cleansed and refreshed by the light. Do you remember playing hide and seek as a very small child? You simply covered your eyes—believing that if you couldn't see, then nobody could see you. Sometimes we make the childish choice to act as if the Lord can't see us when we look at things that are not good for us. At that moment, the Evil One is lurking to whisper that the bad thing is really good and won't hurt us. We close the blinds, and darkness begins to fill us.

Yet our wonderful Lord keeps knocking at the door. Contrary to the lies of the Devil, the Lord understands. Nothing can separate us from His searching love, not even closed blinds and filthy eyes. We may have blown it with bad eyes and souls filled with darkness, but all who call on the name of the Lord will be saved!

Have you been looking at the wrong stuff? Are you all gunked up? Guess what? His eyes are clear and shining with love for you, His heart ready to forgive and cleanse.

Let Him. Let Him clean you out and help you learn to have eyes only for Him and His good stuff. Make a covenant with your eyes to only look at the good stuff of life.

Letting Jesus Lead You

Job 31:1 says, "I made a covenant with my eyes not to look lustfully at a young woman." I heard Sergio Scataglini once teach on the "second second." It's a practical way to live out a covenant with your eyes. If your eyes inadvertently alight on a sexually provocative image, turn your eyes away by the second second. The first second, when the image comes into our view, is not sinful but merely tempting. It is in the second second that we decide whether to let darkness in through our eyes. This applies to everything that is not good for us.

Without fear or condemnation, learn the habit of not letting the bad stuff into your eyes, your ears, or your minds. Garbage in, garbage out! Remember you are a child of God. Learn to rest from input like junk media, junk talk, junk music, junk thinking that you wouldn't let a small child experience. You'll be free and clear for the Holy Spirit to fill to overflowing with wonder-working power!

You really can experience *His* pleasure, *His* security, *His* control—and become full of His light all the time. Let Him clear your eyes and your heart of unrepentant sin—and you'll find yourself moving mountains at His leading!

CHAPTER 24

THE ACCIDENTAL OMELET

And we know that God causes everything to work together for the good of those who love God and are called according to his purpose for them.

— *Romans 8:28*

It has become a delightful habit to make a simple breakfast for my wife each morning: scrambled eggs, toast, juice, and coffee. As people often do, I have moved from experimentation to "getting it down to a science" to "ritual!" Here are the "sacred steps:"

Step one: Turn stove to medium, place pan on stove, pour in olive oil.

Step two: Place eggs in bowl and add milk, grated cheddar cheese, salt and pepper.

Step three: Beat together, pour into pan, and let it cook awhile before scrambling.

Step four: Make toast, pour juice and coffee, set out plates and silverware.

Step five: Scramble eggs with spatula and serve.

LETTING JESUS LEAD YOU

One morning the "ritual" got scrambled! Several distractions happened between steps three and five. Before I knew it, the toast had popped up and was rapidly cooling when I realized the eggs were "beyond their time." I hastily grabbed the spatula to begin scrambling the solid mass and unintentionally flipped half of the egg and cheddar mixture over onto the other half, creating a perfect, accidental omelet! I went from "messed up" to "blessed up" in an instant!

In learning to rest in His love in all the ups and downs of life, sometimes we need to recall the times God has turned things around for us when everything was falling apart.

Take a look at this situation recorded in Mark, in which the disciples went from "messed up" to "blessed up"!

> But soon a fierce storm arose. High waves began to break into the boat, until it was nearly full of water. Jesus was sleeping at the back of the boat with his head on a cushion. Frantically they woke him up, shouting, "Teacher, don't you even care that we are going to drown?" When he woke up, he rebuked the wind and said to the waves, "Quiet down!" Suddenly the wind stopped, and there was a great calm. Then he asked them, "Why are you so afraid? Do you still not have faith in me?" And they were filled with awe and said among themselves, "Who is this man, that even the wind and waves obey him?" (Mark 4:37–41)

Storms are hard. Have you ever sailed into a spiritual, emotional, physical, relational, vocational, or financial storm?

Entering a storm may at first be exhilarating, then alarming, then terrifying. When you are in the middle of a storm, it seems to last forever and may bring much heaviness, depression, and despair. Have you ever noticed that coming out of a storm is a sudden thing? Suddenly the wind dies down, the sun comes out, the waves calm, and secure land comes into sight. The "suddenly" happens so fast that it takes you a while to let go and rest again in the calm and the light.

As we look backward from the sun-splashed beach and reflect on lessons learned, such "storms" can be considered precious times of life. With enough time and openness to the Lord, deep pain and weariness from storms will give way to even deeper wisdom, healing, gratitude, and joy.

HOWEVER, when you are in the storm, there is a lot more perspiration than perspective! The Lord understands this. That is why He spoke this through Paul, the great persecutor who became greatly persecuted: "I am convinced that nothing can ever separate us from God's love" (Rom. 8:38). He was speaking to believers. Stop and think about this. When you let the Lord in, nothing that comes at you from the outside will drive Him out! Ponder that. Give thanks!

Paul said at the opening of his letter to the Roman believers that he was looking forward to seeing them for the first time. He had planned to come to them many times in the past but had been prevented. By what? Stormy trials. Through all the hellish battles he had to endure, Paul became convinced *that the Lord* was unshakeable. Are you convinced? If so, rejoice. If not, ask the Lord to convince you! Have a real, open-hearted conversation with Him that leads to convincing. I am convinced that Paul became convinced through wide-open, blunt, heart-rending conversations with the Lord in every up and down circumstance. (We know it was a confrontational interchange even on the road to Damascus that began Paul's relationship with the Lord.) Notice that the root word of *confidence* is "confide." I'm struck by the fact that after all his trials, Paul's confidence was not found in signs and wonders but, like Elijah in 1 Kings 19, was found in frail encounters with "the still small voice."

Letting Jesus Lead You

In 2 Corinthians, Paul pours his gut out, pleading three times for the Lord to remove the "thorn" of a painful challenge. Each time the Lord answered, "My grace is all you need. My power works best in your weakness." In the storm, in the mess, when you pour out all you have to Him, He'll help you'll realize that He's all you have and all you need. The key is true, gut-wrenching conversation, crying out in one's weakness during the storm. Look at what Paul was able to say after he gave himself to the Lord's embrace: *"Therefore most gladly I will rather boast in my infirmities, that the power of Christ may rest upon me"* (2 Cor. 12:9). How wonderfully ironic! As I declare my weakness, He reveals that His love is sufficient for me. My wholeness does not come by pulling myself together but by letting Him hold me in my mess. Try it. His hands will flip you from messed up to blessed up!

With Jesus, victory is never an accident! Wonderful omelets are not accidental to Him who slept like a baby when all hell was breaking loose. Jesus disarmed hell's grip on you, so rest in His.

CHAPTER 25

THE CONTINUING STORM

Jesus was sleeping at the back of the boat with his head on a cushion. The disciples woke him up, shouting, "Teacher, don't you care that we're going to drown?"

—*Mark 4:38*

Kim and I once went away to a pastors and spouses retreat in the midst of a stormy time of ministry. Even though we had experienced many years of profound spiritual growth and revelation, we were nonetheless weary and wounded from trying *so hard* for years to help conflicted congregations in a sea of shifting denominational politics. We had specific questions to ask the Lord. Should we go to the new assignment offered by our denominational leaders? Or, should we retire from leading congregations and step out in faith to begin Come Rest Ministries?

The second day we gave ourselves to a self-guided retreat. The guidebook offered us three options of Scripture passages. Not coincidentally, we both selected the storm-tossed passage from Mark 4 (discussed in the previous chapter). The guidebook suggested we open ourselves to the Lord by meditating on the passage with a method practiced by Ignatius of Loyola.

Letting Jesus Lead You

This method is a wonderful way to become more confident in hearing the voice of the Lord.

> 1. Put yourself in the place of one of the characters in a Bible story and immerse yourself in the action. Consider the external circumstances according to your five senses. Consider your internal feelings, thoughts, and reactions. Identify with the character from their point of view toward the Lord.

> 2. After some significant time of resting in God through this process (at least 30 minutes), begin a conversation with the Lord. Ask the Lord if He has anything to say.

> 3. Take time to learn to hear His voice in your heart and write what you hear in a prayer journal.

Prayer journaling is a wonderful way to converse confidently with the Lord. Consider it a "Dear Lord" diary. Simply begin every entry with one of His names and write to Him. Then pause and listen in your heart. He says quite simply in John 10:27, "My sheep hear My voice" (NASB). So write down the thoughts, pictures, or Scriptures that come to you. Ponder them. If they are in line with Scripture, if they show Jesus' heart by lining up with the fruit of the Spirit, and if they reasonably relate to your situation—you can be confident those thoughts are from the Lord.

Galatians 5:22–23 says the fruit of the Spirit are love, joy, peace, patience, kindness, goodness, faithfulness, gentleness, and self-control. These fruit express the heart of Jesus.

The Lord never speaks contrary to His written words in the Bible. Everything He says in your heart is intended to lead you to express more of the nine fruit in your life. Look for a connection between the Scripture, your journal conversation, your need, and the nine fruit. The Lord will help you connect the dots to know what to do in your situation to become more like Him. We often wonder in our weakness what the Lord is up to. Whatever it is in life, it is always about Jesus, His love for you, and His desire to lead you to become more like Him.

That morning, immersing myself in the fourth chapter of Mark, I closed my eyes and saw myself as one of the twelve disciples, specifically one of the fisherman.

We set out on the lake, and I feel confident—I am a fisherman, used to boats and lakes—just as a pastor is confident in the trappings of church life. I savor the warm sun and the cool breeze on my face. I taste occasional sea spray. Sea gulls hover nearby. I'm actually free to enjoy their antics instead of warily shooing them away from our usual catch of fish. The boat gently cuts through subtle waves with my friends' conversation as background noise. I see Jesus lying down at the back of the boat for an afternoon siesta. His head hits the small cushion and He is fast asleep (a little peace after a lot of ministry). One could almost go to sleep standing up with the gentle rocking of the boat...

...Suddenly the wind shifts gear. A storm is brewing, and a sense of excitement is giving way to alarm. I glance over at Jesus and think, "Master, your nap is history!" A big fat wave slops over the boat and almost knocks me over. I'm glad for my sea legs. Whoosh! The next wave puts me flat. The sun is gone and the rain is vertical, stinging, cutting. Everyone is holding on for dear life. The boat is filling up with water. I look to see where the Master has gone. You've got to be kidding me! Still asleep!

The boat is almost full to overflowing. Someone cries out the exact thing I'm thinking, "Master don't you care we are perishing?" The question rolls around and around in my mind, "Don't you care?" Then I notice something that pulls laughter out of me: Jesus' head on the cushion and the waves lapping up on His cheeks! Hilarious! Not a care in the world...

That's when my meditation shifted from the story back to my room, and then my journal conversation began with the Lord.

Letting Jesus Lead You

In all my years in the ministry, I was never struck with the hilarity of Jesus sleeping in rising water! It's one thing for the landlubbers of the twelve to be uptight in the storm, but when the fisherman were scared to death and they all saw Him *continuing* to sleep—it's too ridiculous to fathom.

Yes the storm was scary, but it was the "continuing" that offended them. It was no big deal to deal with a storm for a little while because, after all, the Master was with them. However, when it became evident it was a killer storm, and it seemed painfully apparent that He didn't *care*—there came a shattering aloneness more overwhelming than any thunderous wave.

Have you ever been in a situation in which it appeared no one cared? Have you ever felt that God doesn't care? The apparent continuing silence of God. Apparent. Continuing.

He showed me how weak I am, how little I can endure when I can't see Him acting, can't hear Him speaking. He showed me how afraid I still am of pain and dying. How, when push comes to shove, I still doubt His promises when I'm under fire or under water too long. How quickly I can be forced into a corner of rejection, fear, and self-pity, crying, "Don't you care?"

Jesus first quieted the storm and then asked this disquieting question: "Why are you so afraid?" Have you ever asked God, *Why?* About your circumstances? Have you ever thought that when you ask Him *why*, He might be answering you with the same question—*why*? "Why are you so afraid?"

Notice that He said "*so* afraid." Being fully human, Jesus understands fear. Yet He was amazed that His closest friends were *so* afraid. Why? The answer lies in His very next question, "Do you *still* have so little faith?" He was saying, "Come on guys, we've come this far together and you are still totally losing it?"

COME REST

Our response to His continuing silence is often to despair that He doesn't care. His response to our desperate lament is to still the storm outside us and start probing the storm inside us.

What is the worst that can happen to you right now in your life? Why does that threaten you? Begin to listen in the storm. Let Him ask you some *Why* questions for a change. In continuing dialogue He will *change you.*

So, confront Him if need be. Ask Him if He doesn't care. Lament to Him. Come to Him. Give Him your burden of despair. He'll confront the storm inside and outside. Let Him put His arm around you and show you the next step He wants you to take.

Most certainly, it is to put your head on the "cushion" of His chest. Before you know it, the storm will pass, and you will be well on your way to learning from Him how to rest peacefully through the next storm. And if, for some reason, you get hysterical in the next storm, He won't laugh or yell at you—He will simply be asking you *Why?*

The storm inside us cannot continue after the child in us starts talking with and trusting in Him.

LET'S PRAY:

Lord, this last storm has gone on too long for me and/or my loved ones. It helps to know You are not worried, but I need your reassurance. I now take my eyes off the storm and turn back to You. Come, Holy Spirit, and find that place inside me where You know I am holding on too tight. Help me now to let go and rest in Your love. Quiet the storm within me. I believe Your Word that we will get "to the other side of the lake" regardless of this storm. I now speak to this storm, "Be quiet, in Jesus' name." Amen.

CHAPTER 26

DIVIDED PORTION SYNDROME

Casting all your care upon Him, for He cares for you.
— *1Peter 5:7, NKJV*

Have you ever been worried and distracted from what really matters? It's like allowing yourself to be diverted from the fresh produce section at the grocery store to keep cramming your cart full of the options in the junk food aisle.

Fortunately, the Lord loves us too much to stand by and let us be consumed by worry and distraction. He is, in fact, a consuming fire, and He offers Himself as the "good portion" upon which to feast with a heart of thanksgiving.

Do you want a life full of the junk food of worry, or a life full of the peace of Jesus?

Worry wearies. Jesus satisfies.

One day the Lord led me to Psalm 61:2. "From the end of the earth I will cry to You, When my heart is overwhelmed; Lead me to the rock that is higher than I" (NKJV). He showed me that He was the "rock that is higher than I." Then He said, "However, you spend a lot of time in recreational anxiety."

Wow! He is there deep within as my "rock," yet I often fail to go to Him and rest in His peace. It's like I know He is there but I so often make the barely conscious, yet intentional, choice to ruminate and dwell in various "mid-level" fears of my circumstances.

On a walk in the woods He once said to me, "Search My Scriptures and find one place where it ever says I am worried about anything!" What a perspective changer! Think about it. Whatever you are worried about as you read this, He is not worried about it at all. He may be hurting for you in your stress, but He is not threatened. He is not concerned that what you are going through might destroy you. He is focused on calling your name... offering to take you to the rock that is higher than you.

> Martha, Martha, you are worried and troubled about many things. But one thing is needed, and Mary has chosen that good part, which will not be taken away from her (Luke 10:41–42, NKJV).

What was going on in that story? Didn't Martha want to do a good thing for Jesus? Of course! But her heart was not in the right place. It wasn't so much that the Lord wanted her to get her body out of the kitchen. He simply wanted to get *her heart* to focus on Him. Because she was so focused on the meal, she was operating only in the strength of her own power. Therefore, her patience wore thin in crankiness with her sister. The project had become more important than the person. And impatience is not a fruit of the Spirit!

Worry is a choice to dwell in fear. *Adoration* is a choice to dwell in the shadow of His wings. Worry is focus on self. Adoration is focus on Jesus.

Adoration of Jesus is total yieldedness to Him. If He has my full attention and wants me to wholeheartedly make a sumptuous meal, then I am free to give myself fully to the preparation of the meal as a labor of love to Him. But Martha had "divided-portion syndrome." Mary, on the other hand, had chosen Jesus as her only portion. When Jesus is all you need, you cannot be jerked around by your emotions, people, or circumstances. If Jesus is all I need, then I have sold out to Him. That means people have nothing I need and therefore I am free to love them with no strings attached. I can, resting in Jesus' love, successfully resist the temptation to manipulate people by my will and I can successfully refrain from taking the bait of their manipulation or offense.

Martha, like most of us, was trying to do something for Jesus. But Mary chose to give something to Jesus. The Lord doesn't need us to do things for Him. He wants us to relate to Him. Every time we choose Him as our portion, our all-in-all, we minister to Him. Start seeing your every circumstance as an opportunity to choose Jesus as your everything. Start seeing everything you do as a way to minister to Jesus. Stop striving to live for Him, and start letting Him live for you! Then you will begin to see your life as simply a grateful response to Him because of all He has done for you! Begin enjoying trusting Him as your portion.

Martha was striving to make a great feast for the Lord more than she was feasting on the Lord in her heart as she worked. Therefore, she was easily distracted by her worry when the meal wasn't coming together.

Although I have prepared some meals throughout twenty-eight years of marriage, my wife Kim fixed most of our family meals. However, in this last year, with some role reversal, I have been making most of the meals. Planning, preparing, and serving a meal for others is not easy work! Sooner or later, the process comes to a crescendo/crisis—just before mealtime. One-too-many pots on burners, one–too-many open cupboards, one-too-many place settings, my non-yielded heart, and not having enough hands—these can set me on the edge, and over it!

If Martha had begun the meal preparation by resting in Jesus' love in her heart, she would never have been jerked around by whatever was not going well in the kitchen. I am learning to ask the Lord to help me make a meal or do whatever task is before me. I'm even learning to ask Him to remind me to lean on Him several times during the task. It's like hitting the "refresh" button for a website! He loves for us to let Him in on what we are doing!

When Jesus does not have my full attention, something else does. It really is all or nothing. Am I attracted to Jesus or distracted from Him? I become more like what I allow myself to be attracted to. Attraction to my own needs and fears becomes distraction from Jesus.

Distraction is choosing to look away from the Lord. These two behaviors work together. When I feel afraid about something, I either choose to bring it to the Lord and look at it with Him or I choose to take it on myself. The moment I take it on, I am distracted from Him. Worry *is* distraction and also opens the door to other distractions. There is not one style of adoration God is seeking. But there is one heart of adoration He is looking for—the yielded heart.

Martha could have adored Jesus from the kitchen just as deeply as Mary adored Him at His knee. The problem was that Martha was not yielded to the Lord, but she was yielded to the work of her own hands. When we are worried and distracted, we will depend on the work of our own hands for our security. And when we depend on our own hands, our eyes will be distracted by anything else we can grasp. Thus, the moment we take our eyes off Jesus, our heart will follow. We become what we treasure, what we adore. He says in Matthew 6:21, "Where your treasure is, there your heart will be also" (NKJV).

Here is a faith exercise you can do whenever you are worried. It's about choosing His re-creative power rather than recreational anxiety. It has helped me when I am tempted to worry. I call it the Path to Peace. Philippians 4:6–7 says,

> Be anxious for nothing, but in everything by prayer and supplication, with thanksgiving, let your requests be made known to God; and the peace of God, which surpasses all understanding, will guard your hearts and minds through Christ Jesus (NKJV).

I love the grace implied in the first phrase, "Worry about nothing." The Lord knows we are weak and struggle with fear. But worry is a choice to dwell in fear. The Lord offers the choice of His road less traveled. When you find yourself afraid or discover you have already been fixating on your problems, stop. Back up if necessary and take the Lord by the hand down His path of peace, as outlined in Philippians 4. Here's the Path to Peace:

Worried? →

Pray →

Give thanks →

Make requests→

Receive His Peace!

The next time you are tempted to worry, cast it all on Him. Talk to Him. Thank Him for every single thing He has done for you. Think to thank! Of course you don't feel like it—that's why He's given you this path! Think of everything you can. Thank Him for making you. Thank Him for loving you. Thank Him for dying on the cross for you. Thank Him for being with you, even when you don't feel His presence. Keep stepping along the path. Think, thank, think, thank…some people might call it counting your blessings, but it's much more than that. It's turning away from fear and running to Him!

After you can't think of any more thanks, pause. Then pour out your whole heart and "ask big." Ask God to fix every single thing you were worried about. Ask Him to do what only He can do. Cast all your cares on Him, and before you know it the Holy Spirit inside you will release His peace like a force field guarding your heart and mind in a way that cannot be explained.

It's always your choice. You can dwell in fear or the shadow of His wings. He offers Himself as the path less traveled. Choose Him as your all in all moment by moment. You'll never suffer from divided portion syndrome again!

CHAPTER 27

HARD TO SAY GOODBYE

Therefore you now have sorrow; but I will see you again and your heart will rejoice, and your joy no one will take from you.
— *John 16:22, NKJV*

I have been a Green Bay Packer fan ever since 1965 when they won the NFL Championship over my dad's favorite team, the Cleveland Browns. I was nine years old. Except for those who grow up in a city with a pro team, most of us become fans for life of teams that were champions when we were children. We all like the winner.

A couple of years ago I went to a coffee counter to get a refill and a woman commented on the logo on my sweatshirt. She exclaimed, "Yeah, Packers! They're my team, too! I'm so relieved we get to have Favre for one more year!" Then she walked away. I thought, "Yes, me too." Why were we so relieved? Because it's hard to say goodbye!

To you non-NFL fans, let me explain. To you fans, hang around, you might enjoy this...or maybe not. I am glad to declare that number four, Brett Favre, is one of my sports heroes. He has been the Green Bay Packers' star quarterback through an incredible unbroken string of games, playing through many injuries, making incredible plays ever since 1992. He has been the league's most valuable player a record three times and led the Packers to victory in the 1997 Super Bowl. He now has almost all records for quarterbacks, and is a sure Hall of Fame inductee. He is known for his relentless boyish love for the game and tough competitive spirit. He has been the face of the NFL for many years, much as was Michael Jordan for the NBA. Of course, I believe he is the best ever. (Settle down, you Peyton Manning and Tom Brady freaks! Come rest in Jesus' love!) Regardless, many fans want to keep holding onto this era. We don't want Brett to retire. We love to watch him play the way he plays. Some say he is aging and fading. We don't care. We want the experience to last.

Of course, if we fans think it is hard, how much harder is it for the athlete to let it end? In each of the last three years there has been much conjecture as to when Brett would retire. Recently, Brett announced he was retiring, then decided to come back. It appears at publication time to be unclear whether the Packers want him or if he will be playing somewhere else. Some fans and commentators think Favre should quit and get on with his life. The fact that Favre's un-retirement is such big news is because it taps into deep emotions regarding change.

When we sense we are near the end of a season of life, there is something in us that wants to hold onto what was. If things change never to return, it is the death of what was. Every ending touches us consciously or subconsciously as a reminder that one day we will die.

There is also something in us that does not like to see fading glory. So we are torn. We want what was, yet we have to admit things are changing. We see things moving into the uncertain future, and we are afraid. Why can't we stay and have goodness not fade?

LETTING JESUS LEAD YOU

That's what was going on with Peter, James, and John. They were Jesus' closest friends, and they accompanied him up onto the mountaintop. They saw Jesus ablaze with the shining glory of God's presence all over his body. They saw Him visiting with Moses and Elijah in a supernatural cloud. Truly awesome! In Matthew 17:4 Peter said to Jesus, "Lord, it is good for us to be here; if You wish, let us make here three tabernacles: one for You, one for Moses, and one for Elijah" (NKJV). Maybe he thought, "This is it. We get to be beamed up to heaven!" Regardless, he must have been more than a little disappointed when the shining faded and Jesus called him to go back down into the valley with Him. They must have seen that determined look in His eye, the same look He had when He was doing all the crazy talk about dying on a cross. He was resting secure in His Father's love, totally ready to lay down His life at the right time. Peter and the boys were neither resting secure nor ready to lay it all down. They wanted to stay on the mountain, not go move one.

We don't like our heroes talking like losers. Peter had been so upset he rebuked the same Lord whom he had just praised as the Christ. Can you imaging chewing Jesus out? In one sense we do that every time we refuse to do as the Lord commands. Jesus turned and rebuked Peter and Satan at the same time, saying, "Satan, get behind me!" Obviously Peter was not Satan, but obviously Satan was on the scene deceiving Peter to set himself against Jesus' mission. We may not rebuke the Lord with our words, but we can passively and aggressively refuse Him by ignoring His sacrificial call and doing our own thing.

We don't like the fading of our heroes. We don't like our heroes to move in a direction that makes us uncomfortable, much less ends the current state of relationship. Soon the disciples would be meeting with Him in an upper room the night before His death. He was preparing them. In John 16

He was saying goodbye. He acknowledged their sorrow but promised them that the ending of their three-year journey with Him was going to bring something even better. They did not believe Him.

We fans don't want Favre to stop playing. Maybe the good old days will return. Yet, we know, sooner or later, he will retire. I wonder, though, how often fans put themselves in the place of their heroes. Is continuing to play what's best for Brett and his family? Is playing what God wants for Brett? Those concerns are far more important than my need to see him play more.

So now, each time I think of Brett I pray, "Thank You, Lord, for all the fun You have brought into my life through the way Brett plays. Lord, I ask You to save Brett if he's not saved. Fill him and his family with Your overflowing love now and forever. Help him live and play to please You, not people. Amen."

That is my prayer in the name of One who is more than my hero. He's the Hero of heroes, the King of kings! It's a prayer worth praying for everyone you know. And because He left the mountaintop for the valley of death for us—His glory will never fade—it will shine *forever*. If you and I will let Him love us, we will shine with Him forever—and no one will take our joy from us...*He promised*.

It's hard to say goodbye until you let go and rest in the truth of the meaning of *goodbye*. It's an old English contraction that means "God-be-with-ye!" If Jesus is with you, loving you and leading you, He will let you know when it's time to let good things go and say goodbye. You can rest in His comforting assurance that, under His watchful eye, good things give way to even better things. Romans 8:2–29 says that "God causes *everything* to work together for the good of those who love God and are called according to His purposes."

Letting Jesus Lead You

Therefore, it is actually a good thing to let good things end. So, thanks for being you, Brett Favre, God be with ye, I pray you will let Him love you and lead you "4-ever!"

Chapter 28

Walkabout!

*Do not worry...look at the birds...consider the lilies...
seek first the kingdom...*
— *Matthew 6, NKJV*

The Lord wants you to take Him so seriously that you stop taking yourself too seriously. He wants you to lighten up. This is nothing superficial.

I think Jesus would have made a good Australian outbacker! In the land "down under," people in the outback like to go on "walkabouts." Basically, you let go of worry and go out in nature to see what you will see. Jesus knows you need to stop worrying even more than you need food and money. What does stop the drain and release His wellspring of love? Look at each day as a walkabout—Jesus' way. An old spiritual word for this is *contemplation*, which is simply walkin' and talkin' with Jesus. Try it.

Letting Jesus Lead You

Therefore I say to you, **do not worry** about your life, what you will eat or what you will drink; nor about your body, what you will put on. Is not life more than food and the body more than clothing? **Look at the birds** of the air, for they neither sow nor reap nor gather into barns; yet your heavenly Father feeds them. Are you not of more value than they? Which of you by worrying can add one cubit to his stature?

So why do you worry about clothing? **Consider the lilies** of the field, how they grow: they neither toil nor spin; and yet I say to you that even Solomon in all his glory was not arrayed like one of these. Now if God so clothes the grass of the field, which today is, and tomorrow is thrown into the oven, will He not much more clothe you, O you of little faith?

Therefore do not worry, saying, 'What shall we eat?' or 'What shall we drink?' or 'What shall we wear?' For after all these things the Gentiles seek. For your heavenly Father knows that you need all these things. But **seek first the kingdom** of God and His righteousness, and all these things shall be added to you. Therefore do not worry about tomorrow, for tomorrow will worry about its own things. Sufficient for the day is its own trouble (Matt. 6:25–34, emphasis mine).

Contemplation is an important part of the lifestyle of rest. Contemplation is not complicated or mysterious. You simply yield your listening heart to the Lord. The more complicated life seems, the simpler the answers Jesus provides. Some people shy away from contemplation because they don't think they are "spiritual enough" or because they think it seems "too mystical." These are misconceptions. True contemplation is simply letting the Lord speak to your heart. Contemplation is Jesus' intimate invitation to see the rest of your life as a walkabout with Him in this garden called earth.

COME REST

Jesus gives us key phrases to teach the four steps of real contemplation: "Do not worry," "Look at the birds," "Consider the lilies," and "Seek first the kingdom."

1. Let go... Do not worry. Worry is holding onto fear, so let go. Some call this centering prayer. It's the "front porch" to contemplation. Ask the Holy Spirit to touch your life. Close your eyes and rest in Him in silence. Trust that He is moving in you to do what needs to be done. Keep letting go. If a thought, image, or feeling rises up within you, trust that He is prying it loose, and let it go into His hands. Let Jesus take your fears. He's not worried, why should you be?

2. Look out... Look at the birds. He means what He says. The next time you are stressed, *get up* and go outside and find some birds! Watch them flit, alight, and fly about. Don't think about anything but the way they live their life. Gaze at some flowers from a distance, then up close. Again, don't think about anything but the way they exist. Experience their intricate detail, fantastic aroma, and varied texture. Let nature be the God-revealing gift that it is.

3. Look in...Consider the lilies. Say, "Lord, speak to my heart." Listen and wait for thoughts, words, phrases, or pictures to come to you. Let Him ask you questions like He does in the verse. And ask Him some questions. Then simply consider whatever surfaces in your mind. Write some things down. Let these things sink in like rain in a garden.

4. Look Up...Seek first the kingdom. Seek after Him. Praise Him with passion. The Bible says He inhabits our praises. His presence draws closer as you praise Him. Praise is honoring Him for who He is (i.e., kind, faithful, holy, loving, wise). Thank Him with passion. Thanks is honoring Him for what He has done (i.e., the cross, resurrection, salvation, life, breath, family, friends). Listen even as you are praising and thanking. He will fuel the fire with more thoughts, praise, and thanks. He will begin to speak counsel to you.

When thoughts come, say them aloud and write them down. Then finish slowly by declaring the Lord's Prayer.

The more you open your heart to Jesus as He commands in Matthew 6:23–35, the more you will live the truly lighthearted life He desires for you.

Matthew 6:25–35 is really the doorway to resting in His love on earth. Jesus can't give you rest until you let go and open yourself to His will, as expressed in these powerful verses.

Lastly and most importantly, consider verse 26: "Are you not of more value than they?"

One morning I was out mowing my lawn and saw a dear neighbor walking nearby with her granddaughter. She is a mighty woman of prayer—such a blessing to us. They stopped and we conversed for a few minutes, easily flowing into a brief time of mutual spiritual encouragement. The Lord spoke to my heart and said, "Tell her that I do not take her for granted." When she heard that, her eyes teared up and she said, "That blesses me more than you know." The Lord knows that about each one of us, doesn't He? That's what's going on in verse 26. He knows.

The Lord knows that, sooner or later, the child within us is going to wonder, *What about me? How will I be provided for? How will I be protected? I'm following You, Lord, but things aren't easy. I'm afraid… I'm afraid that you have forgotten and don't care as much about me as I thought.*

And so He asks us to go on a walkabout and compare our value to the birds and flowers. To Him it's not even close! Yet, He knows we sometimes feel taken for granted by others and we sure don't want to believe that's true with Him. That's why He wants us to take contemplative walks with Him in nature. He draws our attention to His loving detail in nature and then takes our face in His hands and speaks unspeakable love to us.

My wife, Kim, once took a walk in the woods in the middle of winter, just after the right kind of snowstorm. She stopped by a stream and looked around, marveling at the hushed beauty of the snowy, frosty trees. She exclaimed, "Lord, You are so beautiful!" And He replied, "Don't you know that *you* are My favorite part of all this?" Suddenly, her beautiful green eyes that had been beholding His beauty in the trees were opened wider to behold the wonder of His love for *her*.

The Lord knows your value. He never takes you for granted. He wants to take you on a walkabout for the rest of your life. Let go. Look out. Look in. Look up! No worries, mate!

CHAPTER 29

SCHEDULED MAINTENANCE

Keep the Sabbath day holy. Don't pursue your own interests on that day, but enjoy the Sabbath and speak of it with delight as the Lord's holy day.

— *Isaiah 58:13*

Speaking of rest... here is one of the Lord's most disruptive and igniting commands of all!

Sabbath is about resting from your labors in His love. Fullness of fruitful resting cannot happen if we ignore this command.

Not resting in the Lord through Sabbath is "I-dolatry." It means I am my own god. It means I buy the lie that I have to take care of me because no one else will—certainly not God. I place myself on the throne of my life, rather than resting in His arms, trusting and loving Him as a child.

Resting in Him begins and ends in Sabbath-keeping, not for legalism but for love. Sabbath-keeping is a "love language" toward the Lord.

Once our daughter, Emily, was off to kindergarten, my wife, Kim, found a special bond with our three-year-old son,

COME REST

Daniel, in ambling walks around the long circular drive of our neighborhood. They had no agenda. They just walked to see what they would see. It was familiar, secure territory with regular landmarks (i.e., "Best Rock" was a boulder perched in a neighbor's landscaping—they always had to stop there for a "climb and perch"). Yet, on each walk there were always new experiences and conversations. One day, Daniel called out, "Mommy, give me a hug—I'm cold!" Of course she obliged. Then, near the end of the walk, he wheeled around and shouted, "Mommy, I need one more hug. But not for the cold... just for the love!"

Choose one day each week to rest from your labors and celebrate the Lord. Do it for *the love!* The key is intentionally honoring the One who rested from creating on the seventh day. Loving gratitude, not fearful rule-keeping, is the heart of obedience.

Think of Sabbath-keeping as planning to treat one day out of seven like it is a walk around the block with your heavenly Father in familiar territory. It will be familiar in that you do nothing that has to do with "making a living" and you can focus your activity on intimate play, worship, and conversation with God. The Lord says to keep the day holy. *Holy* simply means "set apart." You set apart one day out of seven to simply hang out with the Lord. You get to have lots of hugs with Him, just for the love.

Can you spend the day with other people? Of course! Just keep your grateful heart focused on the Lord and treat people as a gift that you enjoy in His presence. Let His love for you flow to others.

Jesus said the Sabbath was made for people, not people made for the Sabbath! He said that in response to being criticized for healing a man on the Sabbath. His accusers were at the ridiculous extreme of Sabbath-keeping out of fear, rather than

Sabbath-keeping for love. Jesus saw Sabbath as a restful walk with His Father. If the walk leads you to people, then enjoy them and help them if they need it.

The beauty of setting one day apart—without doing anything to sustain your own life—is that you become more aware during the other six days that He is sustaining you on those days as well. The more that I rest from my labors on the Sabbath, the more I realize He is always laboring for me—He is the sustainer of my life—I can trust Him at all times. Sabbath-keeping is like a governor on my engine. It's God's way of keeping me from burning out. On the Sabbath I exchange hugs with God "just for the love," and He teaches me more and more that all I really need is His love. On the Sabbath I renew my pledge of trust in the Lord, and He renews me! If a car needs an oil change every three thousand miles, a human needs a day set apart with the Lord every seven days. More importantly, if God Himself chose to rest from creation on the seventh day, who do I think I am to not do the same?

It's ironic that parents will encourage their teenagers to get jobs to teach them responsibility and then encourage the teens to take job hours the one day of the week they could take a Sabbath, effectively ignoring God's command. A student's "job" is school. Therefore, homework should be rested from on one day out of seven. In hectic American culture, Sundays have become another day of exhaustion for so many who rely on it to catch up on everything from the past week. Children and youth learn this compulsive cycle quickly. The fact is, our sin nature will lead us around by the nose trying to pack as much activity and productivity as possible into each week. We will take as much time as we have to so we can do what needs to get done.

Sabbath-keeping is God's gift to us to break free and let Him have control over our schedule and pace. If I yield to

Him and set apart a 24-hour period without work for pay or schoolwork, He will empower me to work smarter, not harder. His way is easy and His burden is light. I have seen Sabbath-keeping actually result in more fruitful productivity during my work week. The Lord is not against honest labor. He is against fearful labor that does not trust Him enough to stop working on a seventh day.

Churches buy into the compulsive pace by packing too much activity into Saturdays and Sundays. Unless there is a true emergency, churches need to put an end to committee meetings and fundraisers on Sabbath days. Remember "less is more." Gather together for honoring God in worship and go out and simply enjoy God, nature, gentle play, people, and quiet. Keep it simple. Consider these steps in Sabbath-keeping:

1. Live for an audience of One all week. Live *with* Jesus. Love people in the path He leads.

2. Delight in worshipping Him with other believers once on the weekend.

3. Invest yourself in a midweek small group of believers who are serious about growing in His love together, praying for the world, and ministering to those who don't know Jesus.

4. Enjoy resting with the Lord every seventh day.

Some feel strongly about observing the Jewish Sabbath from Friday sundown to Saturday sundown. Others feel strongly that historical Christianity came to make Sunday (the Lord's resurrection day) its Sabbath observance.

LETTING JESUS LEAD YOU

I believe the Lord is calling us to rest from legalism, controversy, and confusion. Let's look at His Word:

> You are trying to earn favor with God by observing certain days or months or seasons or years. I fear for you (Gal. 4:10–11).

> Some think one day is more holy than another day, while others think every day is alike. You should each be fully convinced that whichever day you choose is acceptable...So let's stop condemning each other. Decide instead to live in such a way that you will not cause another believer to stumble and fall... So then, let us aim for harmony in the church and try to build each other up (Rom. 14:5, 13, 19).

When I look at these passages about the freedom the Lord has given us, it is clear that He wants us to allow each other breathing room regarding our choices for Sabbath rest. Since Jesus tells us He did not come to abolish but fulfill the law, we know that it is still His desire for us to rest in His love with Sabbath celebrating. But we are to keep the Sabbath to lovingly honor the Lord, *not* to find favor with Him. We don't have to perform to find favor with God; He gives us unmerited favor through faith in Jesus.

Sabbath is His loving gift for our renewal, not a burden to divide us. We need to rest both from doctrinal quarreling about Sabbath and foolish disregard of His command—We need to just do it, according to the Lord's leading. Sabbath is not optional, but He does give us freedom to choose when. If we choose not to rest in Sabbath, He will simply stand by, waiting for us to burn out, ever calling our hearts to enjoy His gift. If we do not rest on the Sabbath, He still loves us, but we miss out on all He wants to give us.

In Isaiah 58:14 the Lord promises to reward our Sabbath keeping. He says the more we keep Sabbath the more delight we will find in Him. It's no wonder that most people don't think God is any fun! They spend no time giving Him a chance to become their delight. The Lord is just waiting to show us how hilarious life can be…resting in Him!

In Isaiah 58:11 the Lord promises us that if we live for Him, our lives will be like a well-watered garden, an ever-flowing spring. Remember the wellspring named Rehoboth that I mentioned in chapter nineteen? Repentance makes "room enough" for the Holy Spirit to well up! In fact, Isaiah 58 is a treasure house of promises from the Lord, if we will rest from self-centeredness and put Him and people in need ahead of ourselves. Take a look at this Scripture. Go on a treasure hunt. There are 10 changes God commands us to make and 15 promises of blessing if we do.

There is no fullness of rest for those who will not *choose* to honor the Lord and rest from their labors one day out of seven.

I remember being deeply convicted many years ago while I was reading a book by Eugene Peterson (Bible translator of *The Message*). He pointed out that, sadly, most pastors ignore and break the Sabbath command every week! He talked about how he and his wife began the practice of taking a weekday for their Sabbath celebration because Sundays were a work day for them. I knew that my wife and I needed to make a similar change.

With my wife working as a homemaker and me as a pastor, we experimented with making Friday our Sabbath day, and that generally worked very well for us for about eleven years. We intentionally changed our thinking and speaking regarding a "day off." We talked to our parishioners about Friday being our Sabbath. It wasn't a day off but a day of rest! Most parishioners were supportive and many made similar changes in their own lives. Most importantly, Kim and I knew we could feel the Lord's pleasure.

LETTING JESUS LEAD YOU

This practice deeply enriched our walk with the Lord and the comprehensive intimacy of our marriage in His love. We enjoyed sleeping a little later, or taking an afternoon nap. We spent time in personal morning devotions, then put on some praise music and worshipped together. We usually took a long walk in nature and enjoyed a picnic or dining out. Sometimes we would enjoy window shopping, a movie, or looking through old picture albums. All day we intentionally celebrated the gift of His presence, salvation, and our marriage physically, emotionally, and spiritually. Sabbath-keeping keeps God's priorities clearly in place.

When the kids got home after school on Friday, they found relaxed, joyful, attentive parents ready to enjoy them in many cherished Friday night family activities. We chose to make Saturdays a combination work/home maintenance day. I would do some church related work if necessary, but otherwise that became our day for home family chores, bill paying, ball games, etc.

A major change in my work rhythm was in completing my sermon for Sunday by Thursday evening. This change, in combination with Friday Sabbath, made a huge difference in our family's peace and joy because I was more relaxed, available, and attentive to the whole family without the sermon preparations "hanging over my head." Of course, sometimes things changed and it didn't work out that way, but the overall effect was that the Lord began to help me rest in His love concerning sermons. Sabbath-keeping helped me yield to the Lord's priorities, and my sermons became more and more a fresh, relaxed word of truth and love for the people. They were less and less filled with any fear of what people might think of me. Sabbath-keeping helped me grow in the fear of the Lord and also set me free from the fear of man!

COME REST

During the last couple of years, my wife has had a variable work schedule and we have had to be more intentional about planning a Sabbath day we can share. Sometimes we have had to celebrate our Sabbaths separately. You can choose your own day. Maybe Sunday will work just fine for you. If not, choose another day. If you are single, you don't have to spend the day in solitude. Enjoy friends, family, and dates as a gift from the Lord! Regardless of when you take your Sabbath, make it a priority to protect time to gather in weekend worship with other believers for the audience of One. Following Christ is deeply personal, but not individualistic. The Father sent the Son to save and adopt many children, many brothers and sisters who are free to gather, rest, and serve...just for the love!

LET'S PRAY:

Lord, thank You for loving me even though I have failed to rest in Sabbath and honor You as much as I could have. Please forgive me. Thank You. Please look at my schedule with me and show me the changes You want so my life can be Your well-watered garden, Your ever-flowing spring. Amen.

CHAPTER 30

SKIPPING STONES

Do not fear, little flock, it is the Father's good pleasure to give you the kingdom.

— *Luke 12:32, NKJV*

Whenever we get near a peaceful body of water, my son, Daniel, (now 21) and I will "throw down" and have a stone-skipping contest. The little boy inside each of us loves to pick just the right smooth stone and send it skipping across the water with joyful glee ascending... once, twice, three times... six times—YESSS!!

One day while in prayer, I had a notion to look at what verse 10:28 of each of the four Gospels had to say. The notion turned out to be a playful prompting from the Lord. (His heart is playful and delights in drawing us into amazing discoveries in His Word. He not only walked on water but must have skipped a few stones, as well!) Enjoy watching His truth unfold as you skip from chapter to chapter. Your Father will have fun leading you!

COME REST

SKIP 1: FEAR ONLY GOD

Matthew 10:28: "Fear only God, who can destroy both soul and body in hell." We are afraid to die. Death is the fear behind every ungodly fear. Jesus is saying, "Surrender your fear and receive deeper truth. There is something worse than being killed in a moment—the destruction of your body and soul in hell forever." Proverbs 9:10 says, "The fear of the Lord is the beginning of wisdom" (NKJV). So our first "skip" across the still waters is learning to *fear Him*, which will chase all other fear away.

...SKIP 2: FOLLOW JESUS

Mark 10:28: "Then Peter began to speak up. 'We've given up everything to follow you.' " He said this after Jesus explained that no one can save themselves. Peter was basically saying, "But Lord, we left everything for you. Don't we get extra credit? What's the upside?" And Jesus said, "Leave everything for Me and receive one hundred times what you left and, oh by the way, persecutions!" (plural!) Jesus sees persecution as a blessing... remember, they can only kill your body! They may kill you because of Him, but like Jesus, you have everything to look forward to—true resurrection! So by skip 2 across those waters, we're *fearing Him* and *following Him*.

... SKIP 3:LOVE GOD AND MAN
WHOLEHEARTEDLY

Luke 10:28: " 'Right!' Jesus told him. 'Do this and you will live!' " In this verse Jesus was responding to a religious expert who quoted the greatest commandments, love God and love your neighbor. Jesus said it simply—love God and everybody with all you have, and you will be fully alive! But the expert, like the rest of us, couldn't keep it simple. He was looking for an out, and he challenged Jesus, "And who is my neighbor?"

He might have thought, *surely Jesus will let us set limits on who really is our neighbor.* Surely not! So Jesus told the story of the Good Samaritan, which is evidence of the importance of fully loving God and *everyone* we come across. So as we bounce across the water again, we not only fear and follow God but also go *all out* in love.

SKIP 4: TRUST JESUS FOREVER

John 10:28: "I give them eternal life…neither shall anyone snatch them out of My hand" (NKJV). The One who holds all the cards, holds us! Jesus was saying, "My Dad is tougher than anyone else, and He gave you to Me, so *no one* can take you away from Me." The "10:28 stone" is ready to sink deep into the still waters of God when we have learned to fear God, follow God, really love, and rest secure in His hand.

Skipping stones on still waters with my son is priceless. But what's even better is knowing that the Good Shepherd lives in us and leads us beside still waters.

Do you want to live a 10:28 life? Do you want your loved ones to live a 10:28 life? Then ask the Father with childlike trust to lead you and your loved ones along His 10:28 path—the path from healthy fear to everlasting life! He will. How does that verse from "Amazing Grace" go?

Twas Grace that taught my heart to fear,
and Grace my fears relieved.
How precious did that Grace appear
the hour I first believed!

Fear not, little flock!

COME REST

P.S. Isn't it interesting that just after John 10:28 the crowd wanted to stone Jesus? Funny thing, He just rested secure in His Father's love, faced them down, and passed through the crowd and all their hate. He skipped their stones…waiting for His cross…so the Father could give us His kingdom.

CHAPTER 31

ALL THE WAY

I myself taught Israel how to walk, leading him along by the hand. But he doesn't know or even care that it was I who took care of him.
— *Hosea 11:3*

Do you remember your first day of kindergarten? My mother prepared me for my first day by taking me by the hand on several "dry runs." We walked the three-block journey from our home to my school several times before the big day.

Then it was time! On that great morning, my mother took me only as far as the sidewalk in front of our house. She kissed me and sent me on my way. I walked to the end of the block, crossed the street, and turned to look back at Mom. She blew me a kiss and I waved goodbye. Soon she was out of sight.

Both excited and scared, I walked the first block. Then I stopped, looked back, and realized I really was alone.

I walked another block, looked back, and began to feel great confidence.

COME REST

When I finally reached the schoolyard, I looked back and felt exhilaration and pride. I had made it on my own! Mrs. White welcomed me lovingly into her room and helped me find a place at a drawing table as other children continued to arrive. Suddenly, I heard the loud screaming of a child being dragged down the hall by his mother. He was the biggest child in the class, and he was bawling all the way. I was a little shaken but felt good that I had made it all the way there by myself. (Or at least that's what I thought!)

Twenty years later, I was recounting that day at a family gathering when my mother asked me, "Would you like to know how it really happened?" To my wonderment, she explained that as soon as I had gone out of sight, she had run through the house, into the backyard, and down the alley. She had then followed me at a distance every step of the way! "The problem was that you kept turning around to look behind you and you almost caught me!" she exclaimed. "Once I had to jump behind a big oak tree and another time I had to dive behind a garage!"

They say today is the first day of the rest of your life. I don't know what your first day of school was like, but try this. Whether you are like me—taking a lot for granted—or like the kid who kicked and screamed, there is One who loves you more than any sacrificing mother. But instead of diving behind a garage, He hung on a cross for you to pay the penalty for your sin, to take on all your diseases. He's always on the job to heal and restore you and make you like Him. He promises to finish what He begins in you.

Going it alone is highly overrated. No matter where you are, what you have done, or what has been done to you, your path led you to this book. Your path has led you to Jesus' invitation: "Come Rest in My Love." Every day is always your "first day" in Him.

LETTING JESUS LOVE YOU

So, Jedidiah, simply begin where you are. Let Jesus love you, and let Jesus lead you…all the way home.

And I am certain that God, who began the good work within you, will continue his work until it is finally finished on the day when Christ Jesus returns.

— Philippians 1:6

About the Author and Come Rest Ministries

Richard Speight has served thirty years in pastoral ministry. He has a B.A. from Creighton University and an M. Div. from the University of Dubuque Theological Seminary. He is known for his passion for Jesus and trusted for his prayerful counsel. Richard and his wife Kim have two children, Emily and Daniel. Richard retired in 2006 after 27 years as a United Methodist pastor, and the Speights now invest their lives in helping people rest in and release Jesus' love.

In Matthew 11 the Lord says, "Come to me… and I will give you rest… learn from me for I am gentle…" In Isaiah 58 He promises to make us a well-watered garden if we honor Him and help broken people. Inspired by these Scriptures, **Come Rest Ministries, Inc.** is a 501(c)(3) non-profit ministry led by Richard and Kim Speight.

Come Rest Ministries helps people learn to rest through resources (books and meditational CDs); encounters (three-hour to three-day events which include heartfelt music, teaching, prayer, and reflection times); retreats; spiritual guidance; training small groups; and consulting for churches, ministries, and leaders. Richard is available to speak in a variety of ministry and secular settings. Come Rest ministries will also soon host Rehoboth Outreach and Retreat Center near Cedar Rapids, Iowa.

More information is available at www.comerest.org.

"Resting in Jesus' love is for every moment. Resting in Him is the most fruitful thing you can do. As you rest in His love, His presence comes to rest on you, and His kingdom advances wherever you go!"

— Richard Speight

LEARN TO REST
WITH THESE COME REST MINISTRIES
AUDIO RESOURCES

On each of these CDs, short reflections and teachings are accompanied by instrumental music to guide you in your "quest for rest." They can be used for devotional times, small group gatherings, or church services. Listen to the whole CD at once, or enjoy the reflections one at a time.

CD 1: COME REST MEDITATIONS
Includes meditations on Jesus' invitation to rest, relieving burdens, forgiveness, identity, and more.

CD 2: REFLECTION ON HIS REAL LOVE
Contains meditations on Grace, the leadership of the Lord in our lives, the discipline of contemplation, how to remain steady in the midst of times of shaking, and more.

To order one or both of these CDs, please send your name and address, the CD number of your choice, and your payment ($10 for one or $15 for both CDs, including shipping and handling) to:

Come Rest Ministries
P.O. Box 11010
Cedar Rapids, IA 52410-1010